SMOKE GETS IN YOUR EYES

Most people go to great lengths to avoid thinking about death, but when Caitlin Doughty — a young woman with a degree in medieval history and a flair for the macabre — took a job at Westwind Cremation & Burial, her morbid curiosity turned into her life's work. Leading us behind the black curtain of her profession, Caitlin takes us into a world of vivid characters (both living and deceased) and bizarre details (exactly how a flaming skull looks) — and explores the funeral practices of historic and contemporary cultures, calling for better ways of dealing with death and our dead.

S

T
(r
wa
resea

- ʳ
  ]
- ʳ
  (
-]
  t
  ]
- ʳ
  ]
- ʳ
  (
- ʳ
  ]

ye
at
ıd
y,
p,
:n
al

You

Every contribution is gratefully received. If you
would like to help support the Foundation or
require further information, please contact:

THE ULVERSCROFT FOUNDATION
The Green, Bradgate Road, Anstey
Leicester LE7 7FU, England
Tel: (0116) 236 4325

website: www.foundation.ulverscroft.com

Born on a balmy August evening on the decidedly un-morbid shores of O'ahu, Hawai'i, Caitlin was an even-tempered, bookish child. After high school, she fled east from her island home to the University of Chicago, where she graduated in medieval history. She recommends her thesis — 'In Our Image: The Suppression of Demonic Births in Late Medieval Witchcraft Theory' — as *the* summer must-read for all lovers of demon sex and the late medieval church. Founder of The Order of the Good Death, which aims to bring the realistic discussion of death back into popular culture, Caitlin currently works as a licensed funeral director/mortician in Los Angeles and is in the process of opening her own alternative funeral service.

Visit her website at:
http://www.orderofthegooddeath.com/members/your-mortician

CAITLIN DOUGHTY

---◆---

SMOKE GETS IN YOUR EYES

And Other Lessons from the Crematorium

Complete and Unabridged

ULVERSCROFT
Leicester

First published in Great Britain in 2015 by
Canongate Books Ltd
Edinburgh

First Large Print Edition
published 2016
by arrangement with
Canongate Books Ltd
Edinburgh

A catalogue record for this book is available
from the British Library.

ISBN 978–1–4448–2688–3

Published by
F. A. Thorpe (Publishing)
Anstey, Leicestershire

Set by Words & Graphics Ltd.
Anstey, Leicestershire
Printed and bound in Great Britain by
T. J. International Ltd., Padstow, Cornwall

This book is printed on acid-free paper

To my dearest friends
So supportive, so gracious
A morbid haiku.

WARNING!
LIMITED ACCESS AREA.
CALIFORNIA CODE OF REGULATIONS
TITLE 16, DIVISION 12
ARTICLE 3
SECTION 1221.

Care and Preparation for Burial.

(a) The care and preparation for burial or other disposition of all human remains shall be strictly private . . .

— *Required funeral establishment warning placard*

Contents

Author's Note

According to a journalist's eyewitness account, Mata Hari, the famous exotic dancer turned World War I spy, refused to wear a blindfold when she was executed by a French firing squad in 1917.

'Must I wear that?' asked Mata Hari, turning to her lawyer, as her eyes glimpsed the blindfold.

'If Madame prefers not, it makes no difference,' replied the officer, hurriedly turning away.

Mata Hari was not bound and she was not blindfolded. She stood gazing steadfastly at her executioners, when the priest, the nuns, and her lawyer stepped away from her.

Looking mortality straight in the eye is no easy feat. To avoid the exercise, we choose to stay blindfolded, in the dark as to the realities of death and dying. But ignorance is not bliss, only a deeper kind of terror.

We can do our best to push death to the margins, keeping corpses behind stainless-steel doors and tucking the sick and dying in hospital rooms. So masterfully do we hide death, you would almost believe we are the first generation of immortals. But we are not. We are all going to die and we know it. As the great cultural anthropologist Ernest Becker said, 'The idea of death, the fear of it, haunts the human animal like nothing else.' The fear of death is why we build cathedrals, have children, declare war, and watch cat videos online at three a.m. Death drives every creative and destructive impulse we have as human beings. The closer we come to understanding it, the closer we come to understanding ourselves.

This book is about my first six years working in the American funeral industry, but I believe you will find considerable crossover with how you handle death across the pond. For those who do not wish to read realistic depictions of death and dead bodies, you have stumbled onto the wrong book. Here is where you check the metaphorical blindfolds at the door. The stories are true and the people are real. Several names and details (but not the salacious ones, promise) have been changed to preserve the privacy of certain individuals and to protect the identities of the deceased.

Shaving Byron

A girl always remembers the first corpse she shaves. It is the only event in her life more awkward than her first kiss or the loss of her virginity. The hands of time will never move quite so slowly as when you are standing over the dead body of an elderly man with a pink plastic razor in your hand.

Under the glare of fluorescent lights, I looked down at poor, motionless Byron for what seemed like a solid ten minutes. That was his name, or so the toe tag hung around his foot informed me. I wasn't sure if Byron was a 'he' (a person) or an 'it' (a body), but it seemed like I should at least know his name for this most intimate of procedures.

Byron was (or, had been) a man in his seventies with thick white hair sprouting from his face and head. He was naked, except for the sheet I kept wrapped around his lower half to protect I'm not sure what. Post-mortem decency, I suppose.

His eyes, staring up into the abyss, had gone flat like deflated balloons. If a lover's eyes are a clear mountain lake, Byron's were a stagnant pond. His mouth twisted open in a silent scream.

'Um, hey, uh, Mike?' I called out to my new boss from the body-preparation room. 'So, I guess I should use, like, shaving cream or . . . ?'

Mike walked in, pulled a can of Barbasol from a metal cabinet, and told me to watch out for nicks. 'We can't really do anything if you slice open his face, so be careful, huh?'

Yes, be careful. Just as I'd been careful all those other times I had 'given someone a shave.' Which was never.

I put on my rubber gloves and poked at Byron's cold, stiff cheeks, running my hand over several days' worth of stubble. I didn't feel anywhere near important enough to be doing this. I had grown up believing that morticians were professionals, trained experts who took care of our dead so the public didn't have to. Did Byron's family know a twenty-three-year-old with zero experience was holding a razor to their loved one's face?

I attempted to close Byron's eyes, but his wrinkled eyelids popped back up like window shades, as if he wanted to watch me perform this task. I tried again. Same result. 'Hey, I don't need your judgement here, Byron,' I said, to no response.

It was the same with his mouth. I could

push it shut, but it would stay closed only a few seconds before falling open again. No matter what I did, Byron refused to act in a manner befitting a gentleman about to get his afternoon shave. I gave up and spurted some cream on his face, clumsily spreading it around like a creepy toddler finger-painting in the *Twilight Zone*.

This is just a dead person, I told myself. Rotting meat, Caitlin. An animal carcass.

This was not an effective motivational technique. Byron was far more than rotting meat. He was also a noble, magical creature, like a unicorn or a griffin. He was a hybrid of something sacred and profane, stuck with me at this way station between life and eternity.

By the time I concluded this was not the job for me, it was too late. Refusing to shave Byron was no longer an option. I picked up my pink weapon, the tool of a dark trade. Screwing up my face and emitting a high-pitched sound only dogs could hear, I pressed blade to cheek and began my career as barber to the dead.

* * *

When I woke up that morning, I hadn't expected to shave any corpses. Don't get me wrong, I expected the corpses, just not the

3

shaving. It was my first day as a crematorium operator at Westwind Cremation & Burial, a family-owned mortuary. Or a family-owned *funeral home*. What you call your local death house depends entirely on what region of North America or the UK you live in. Mortuary, funeral home, po-tay-to, po-tah-to. Places for the dead.

I leapt out of bed early, which I never did, and put on pants, which I never wore, along with steel-toed boots. The pants were too short and the boots too big. I looked ridiculous, but in my defence, I did not have a cultural reference point for proper dead-human-burning attire.

The sun rose as I walked out of my apartment on Rondel Place, shimmering over discarded needles and evaporating puddles of urine. A homeless man wearing a tutu dragged an old car tyre down the alley, presumably to repurpose it as a makeshift toilet.

When I first moved to San Francisco, it had taken me three months to find an apartment. Finally, I met Zoe, a lesbian criminal-justice student offering a room. The two of us now shared her bright-pink duplex on Rondel Place in the Mission District. Our home sweet alley was flanked on one side by a popular taqueria and on the other by Esta

Noche, a bar known for its Latino drag queens and deafening ranchera music.

Making my way down Rondel to the BART station, a man across the alley opened his coat to show me his penis. 'Whatcha think of this, honey?' he said, waving it triumphantly at me.

'Well, man, I think you're going to have to do better,' I replied. His face fell. I'd lived on Rondel Place for a year by now. He really *would* have to do better.

From the Mission Street stop, the BART train carried me under the Bay to Oakland and spat me out a few blocks from Westwind. The sight of my new workplace, after a ten-minute trudge from the BART station, was underwhelming. I'm not sure exactly what I was expecting the mortuary to look like — probably my grandmother's living room, equipped with a few fog machines — but from outside the black metal gate, the building seemed hopelessly normal. Eggshell-white, only a single storey, it could have doubled as an insurance office.

Near the gate, there was a small sign: please ring bell. So, summoning my courage, I complied. After a moment, the door creaked open, and Mike, the crematorium manager and my new boss, emerged. I had met him only once before and had been tricked into thinking he was totally harmless — a balding white man in his forties of normal height and weight, wearing a pair of khaki pants. Somehow, in spite of his affable khakis, Mike managed to be terrifying, assessing me sharply from behind his glasses, taking inventory on just how big a mistake he had made in hiring me.

'Hey, morning,' he said. 'Hey' and 'morning' were flat, indistinguishable, under his breath, as if they were meant for only him to hear. He opened the door and walked away.

After a few awkward moments I decided he intended me to follow, and I stepped through the entryway and turned several corners. A dull roar echoed through the hallways, growing louder.

The building's nondescript exterior gave way at the back to a massive warehouse. The roaring was coming from inside this cavernous room — specifically from two large, squat machines sitting proudly in the centre like the Tweedledum and Tweedledee of death. They were made of matching corrugated metal with chimneys that stretched upward and out of the roof. Each machine had a metal door that slid up and down, the chomping mouths of an industrial children's fable.

These are the cremation machines, I thought. There are people in there right now — *dead* people. I couldn't actually see any of these dead people yet, but just knowing they were nearby was exhilarating.

'So these are the cremation machines?' I asked Mike.

'They take up the whole room. You'd be pretty surprised if these *weren't* the machines, wouldn't you?' he replied, ducking through a nearby doorway, abandoning me once again.

What was a nice girl like me doing in a body-disposal warehouse like this? No one in her right mind would choose a day job as a corpse incinerator over, say, bank teller or kindergarten teacher. And it might have been easier to be hired as a bank teller or kindergarten teacher, so suspicious was the death industry of the twenty-three-year-old woman desperate to join its ranks.

I had applied for jobs concealed by the glow of my laptop screen, guided by the search terms 'cremation,' 'crematorium,' 'mortuary,' and 'funeral.' The reply to my job enquiries — if I received any reply at all — was, 'Well, do you have any cremation experience?' Funeral homes seemed to *insist* on experience, as if corpse-burning skills were available to all, taught in your average high-school woodwork class. It took six months and buckets of résumés and 'Sorry, we found someone better qualified' before I was hired at Westwind Cremation & Burial.

My relationship with death had always been complicated. Ever since childhood, when I found out that the ultimate fate for all humans was death, sheer terror and morbid curiosity had been fighting for supremacy in my mind. As a little girl I would lie awake for *hours* waiting for my mother's headlights to appear in the driveway, convinced that she was lying broken and bloody on the side of the highway, flecks of shattered glass stuck to the tips of her eyelashes. I became 'functionally morbid,' consumed with death, disease, and darkness yet capable of passing as a quasi-normal schoolgirl. In college I dropped the pretense, declared my major as medieval history, and spent four years devouring academic papers with names like 'Necro-Fantasy & Myth: Interpretation of Death Amongst the Natives of Pago Pago' (Dr. Karen Baumgartner, Yale University, 2004). I was drawn to all aspects of mortality — the bodies, the rituals, the grief. Academic papers had provided a fix, but they weren't enough. I wanted the harder stuff: real bodies, real death.

Mike returned, pushing a squeaky-wheeled gurney bearing my first corpse.

'There's no time to learn the cremation machines today, so you can do me a favour. Give this guy a shave,' he requested, nonchalant. Apparently the dead man's family wanted to see him one more time before he was cremated.

Motioning for me to follow, Mike wheeled the gurney into a sterile white room just off the crematorium, explaining that this was where the bodies were 'prepared.' He walked over to a large metal cabinet and pulled out a pink plastic disposable razor. Handing it to me, Mike turned and left, disappearing for the third time. 'Good luck,' he called over his shoulder.

As I said, I hadn't expected the corpse shaving, but there I was.

Mike, though absent from the preparation room, was watching me closely. This was a test, my introduction to his harsh training philosophy: sink or swim. I was the new girl who had been hired to burn (and occasionally shave) corpses, and I would either (a) be able to handle it or (b) not be able to handle it. There was to be no hand-holding, no learning curve, no trial period.

Mike returned a few minutes later, stopping to glance over my shoulder. 'Look, here . . . no, in the direction his hair was growing. Short strokes. Right.'

When I wiped the last bits of shaving cream from Byron's face, he looked like a newborn babe, not a nick or razor burn in sight.

Later that morning, Byron's wife and daughter came to see him. Byron was wheeled into Westwind's viewing room and draped in white sheets. A floor lamp fitted with a rose-coloured lightbulb cast a calm glow over his exposed face — far more pleasant than the harsh fluorescent bulbs in the preparation room.

After my shave, Mike had worked some kind of funerary magic to close Byron's eyes and gaping mouth. Now, under the rose lighting, the gentleman seemed almost serene. I kept expecting to hear cries from the viewing room of 'Dear *God*, who shaved him like this!' but to my relief, none came.

I learned from his wife that Byron had been an accountant for forty years. A fastidious man, he probably would have appreciated the close shave. Towards the end of his battle with lung cancer he couldn't get out of bed to use the bathroom, let alone wield a razor.

When his family left, it was time to cremate him. Mike rolled Byron into the mouth of one of the behemoth cremation machines and turned the dials on the front panel with an impressive dexterity. Two hours later, the metal door rose again and revealed Byron's bones, reduced to glowing red embers.

Mike brought me a metal pole with a flat

rake on the end. He demonstrated the long strokes required to pull the bones from the machine. As what remained of Byron fell into the waiting container, the phone rang. It boomed loudly through the speakers in the ceiling, installed specifically to be heard over the thunder of the machines.

Mike tossed me his goggles and said, 'You finish raking him out. I gotta grab the phone.'

As I scraped Byron's body out of the cremation machine, I saw that his skull was still fully intact. Looking over my shoulder to see if anyone, living or dead, was watching, I carefully inched it towards me. When it was near enough to the front of the chamber, I reached down and picked it up. The skull was still warm, and I could feel its smooth, dusty texture through my industrial-grade gloves.

Byron's lifeless eye sockets stared up at me as I tried to remember what his face had looked like as he slid into the flames just two hours before. It was a face I should have known well after our barber-client relationship. But that face, that human, was gone. Mother Nature, as Tennyson said, is 'red in tooth and claw,' demolishing every beautiful thing she has ever created.

Bones, reduced to just their inorganic elements by cremation, become very brittle. As I turned the skull to the side for a better look, the entire thing crumbled in my hand, the shards tumbling into the container through my fingers. The man who was Byron — father, husband, and accountant — was now entirely in the past tense.

I got home that evening to find my roommate, Zoe, on the couch, sobbing. She was brokenhearted over the married man she had fallen for on a recent backpacking trip to Guatemala (a blow to both her ego and her lesbianism).

'How was your first day?' she asked through her tears.

I told her about Mike's silent judgement, about the introduction to corpse shaving, but decided not to tell her about Byron's skull. That was my secret, along with the strange, perverse power I had felt in that moment as skull crusher of the infinite universe.

As the sound of ranchera music from Esta Noche blasted me to sleep, I thought of the skull lodged in my own head. How it would one day emerge after everything that could be recognised as Caitlin — eyes, lips, hair, flesh — was no more. My skull might be crushed too, fragmented by the gloved hand of some hapless twentysomething like me.

Puppy Surprise

My second day at Westwind I met Padma. It wasn't that Padma was gross. 'Gross' is such a simple word, with simple connotations. Padma was more like a creature from a horror film, cast in the lead role of 'Resurrected Voodoo Witch.' The mere act of looking at her body lying in the cardboard cremation container caused internal fits of 'Oh my God. *Holy* — what is — *what* am I doing here? What is this shit? Why?'

Racially, Padma was Sri Lankan and North African. Her dark complexion, in combination with advanced decomposition, had turned her skin pitch-black. Her hair hung in long, matted clumps, splayed out in all directions. Thick, spidery white mould shot out of her nose, covering half her face, stretching over her eyes and yawning mouth. The left side of her chest was caved in, giving the impression that someone had removed her heart in some elaborate ritual.

Padma was in her early thirties when she was felled by a rare genetic disease. Her body was kept for months at the Stanford University Hospital so doctors could run tests to understand the condition that killed her. By the time she arrived at Westwind, her body had taken a turn for the surreal.

Grotesque as Padma appeared in my amateur's eyes, I couldn't shrink away from her body like a wobbly fawn. Mike the crematorium manager had made it clear that I was not being paid to be freaked out by dead bodies. I was desperate to prove that I could share his clinical detachment.

Spiderweb face mould, is it? Oh yes, seen it a million times before, surprised this is such a mild case, really, I would say, with the authority of a true death professional.

Until you've seen a dead body like Padma's, death can seem almost glamorous. Imagine a Victorian consumption victim, expiring with a single trickle of blood sliding from the corner of her rosy mouth. When Edgar Allan Poe's love, Annabel Lee, is taken by the chill of death and entombed, the lovelorn Poe cannot stay away. He goes to 'lie down by the side, of my darling — my darling — my life and my bride, in her sepulchre there by the sea, in her tomb by the sounding sea.'

The exquisite, alabaster corpse of Annabel Lee. No mention of the ravages of decomposition that would have made lying down next to her a rancid embrace for the broken-hearted Poe.

It wasn't just Padma. The day-to-day realities of working at Westwind were more savage than I had anticipated. My days began at eight thirty a.m. when I turned on Westwind's two 'retorts' — industry jargon for cremation machines. I carried a retort-turnin'-on cheat sheet with me for the first month, clumsily cranking the 1970s science-fiction dials to light up the bright-red, blue, and green buttons that set temperatures and ignited burners and controlled airflow. The moments before the retorts roared to life were some of the quietest and most peaceful of the day. No noise, no heat, no pressure, just a girl and a selection of the newly deceased.

Once the retorts came to life, the peace vanished. The room turned into an inner ring of hell, filled with hot, dense air and the rumbling of the devil's breath. What looked like puffy silver spaceship lining covered the walls of the crematorium, soundproofing the room and preventing the rumble from reaching the ears of grieving families in the nearby chapel or arrangement rooms.

The machine was ready for its first body when the temperature inside the brick chamber of the retort reached 816°C. Every morning Mike stacked several State of California disposition permits on my desk, telling me who was on deck for the day's cremations. After selecting two permits, I had to locate my victims in the 'reefer' — the walk-in body-refrigeration unit where the corpses waited. Through a cold blast of air I greeted the stacks of cardboard body boxes, each labelled with full names and dates of death. The reefer smelled like death on ice, an odour difficult to pinpoint but impossible to forget.

The people in the reefer would probably not have hung out together in the living world. The elderly black man with a myocardial infarction, the middle-aged white mother with ovarian cancer, the young Hispanic man who had been shot just a few blocks from the crematorium. Death had brought them all here for a kind of United Nations summit, a round-table discussion on non-existence.

Walking into the body fridge, I made a modest promise to a higher deity that I'd be a better person if the deceased was not at the bottom of a stack of bodies. This particular morning, the first cremation permit was for a Mr. Martinez. In a perfect world, Mr. Martinez would have been right on top, waiting for me to roll him directly onto my hydraulic gurney. To my great annoyance I found him stacked below Mr. Willard, Mrs.

Nagasaki, *and* Mr. Shelton. That meant stacking and restacking the cardboard boxes like a game of body-fridge Tetris.

When at last Mr. Martinez was man-oeuvred onto the gurney, I could proceed with the short trip to the cremation chamber. The last obstacles on the journey were the thick strips of plastic (also popular in car washes and meat freezers) that hung from the doorframe of the reefer, trapping the cold air inside. The strips were my enemy. They entangled everyone who passed through, like spooky branches in the cartoon version of *The Legend of Sleepy Hollow*. I hated touching them, as I imagined that clinging to the plastic were hordes of bacteria and, it stood to reason, the tormented souls of the departed.

If you got caught in the strips, you would inevitably miscalculate the angle needed to roll the gurney out the door. As I gave Mr. Martinez a push, I heard the familiar *thunk* as I overshot and slammed the gurney into the metal doorframe.

Mike happened upon me thunking away, pulling Mr. Martinez back and forth and back and forth and back and forth as he walked by, heading to the preparation room. 'You need help? You got it?' he asked, one eyebrow arched significantly higher than the other, as if to say, *It's painfully obvious how much you don't got it.*

'Nope, I got it!' I replied cheerfully, brushing the bacteria tentacle from my face and heaving the gurney into the crematorium.

I made sure my response was *always* 'Nope, got it!' Did I need help watering the plants in the front courtyard? 'Nope, got it!' Did I need further instructions on how to lather up a man's hand to slip a wedding ring over his bloated knuckle? 'Nope, got it!'

With Mr. Martinez safely out of the reefer, it was time to open the cardboard box. This, I had discovered, was the best part of my job.

I equate opening the boxes with the early '90s stuffed toy for young girls, Puppy Surprise. The commercial for Puppy Surprise featured a group of five-to-seven-year-old girls crowded around a plush dog. They would shriek with delight as they opened her plushy stomach and discovered just how many stuffed baby puppies lived inside. Could be three, could be four, or even five! This was, of course, the 'surprise.'

Such was the case with dead bodies. Every time you opened the box you could find anything from a ninety-five-year-old woman who died peacefully under home hospice care to a thirty-year-old man they found in a dumpster behind a Home Depot after eight days of putrefaction. Each person was a new adventure.

If the body I found in the box was on the unusual side (think: Padma's face mould), my own curiosity led me to gumshoe-style investigations via the electronic death registration system, coroner's amendments, and the death certificate. These bureaucratic necessities would contain more information about the person's life and, more important, their death. The story of how they came to leave the living and join me at the crematorium.

Mr. Martinez was not so out of the ordinary as far as corpses went. Only a three-puppy body, I'd say, if pressed to give him a rating. He was a Latino gentleman in his late sixties who had probably died of a heart condition. Raised up under his skin I could see the outline of a pacemaker.

Legend among crematorium workers holds that the lithium batteries inside pacemakers explode in the cremation chamber if not removed. These tiny bombs have the potential to blow the faces off poor innocent crematorium operators and do damage to the machines. The threat is even greater in the UK, where the operators often do not open the sealed coffins, and just have to go with God and hope they aren't setting up an unplanned fireworks show. I went back to the preparation room for one of the embalmer's scalpels to remove it.

I touched the scalpel to Mr. Martinez's chest and attempted two slices above the pacemaker in a crosshatch pattern. The scalpel looked sharp, but it did nothing to pierce his skin — not even a scratch.

It is not hard to understand why medical schools use cadavers to practise operating techniques, desensitizing their students to the process of causing pain. Performing this mini operation, I felt Mr. Martinez must surely be in agony. Our human identification with the dead always makes us feel like the decedent must be in pain, even though the murk in this man's eyes told me he had long left the proverbial building.

Mike had showed me how to perform a pacemaker removal the week before, but he had made it look easy. It requires more force with the scalpel than you'd think; human skin is surprisingly tough material. I apologised to Mr. Martinez for my incompetence. After several more unsuccessful scalpel jabs and frustrated noises, the metal of the pacemaker revealed itself beneath the lumpy yellow tissue of his chest. With one quick pull it was free.

Now that Mr. Martinez had been identified, relocated, and stripped of all potentially explosive batteries, he was ready to meet his fiery end. I plugged the conveyor belt into the retort and pushed the button, which starts the assembly-line process of rolling a body into the machine. Once the metal door clunked closed I returned to the science-fiction dials at the front of the machine, adjusted the air flow, and turned on the ignition burners.

There is very little to do while a body is burning. I kept watch on the machine's changing temperature and opened the metal door a few inches in order to peek inside and monitor the body's progress. The heavy door creaked when it opened. I imagined it saying, *Beware of what you shall discover, my pretty.*

Four thousand years ago, the Hindu Vedas described cremation as necessary for a trapped soul to be released from the impure dead body. The soul is freed the moment the skull cracks open, flying up to the world of the ancestors. It is a beautiful thought, but if you are not used to watching a human body burn, the scene can be borderline hellish.

The first time I peeked in on a cremating body felt outrageously transgressive, even though it was required by Westwind's protocol. No matter how many heavy-metal album

21

covers you've seen, how many Hieronymus Bosch prints of the tortures of Hell, or even the scene in *Indiana Jones* where the Nazi's face melts off, you cannot be prepared to view a body being cremated. Seeing a flaming human skull is intense beyond your wildest flights of imagination.

When the body goes into the retort, the first thing to burn is its cardboard box, or 'alternative container' as it's called on the funeral bill. The box immediately melts into flames, leaving the body defenceless against the inferno. Then the organic material burns away, and a complete change overtakes the body. Almost 80 per cent of a human body is water, which evaporates with little trouble. The flames then go to work on the soft tissues, charring the whole body a crispy black. Burning these parts, the ones that visually identify you, takes the bulk of the time.

It would be a lie to say I hadn't had a particular vision of being a crematorium operator. I expected the job would involve placing a body in one of the giant machines and settling down with my feet up to eat strawberries and read a novel as the poor man or woman was cremated. At the end of the day I'd take the train home in thoughtful reverie, having come to some deeper understanding of death.

After a few weeks at Westwind, any dreams I had of berry-eating reveries were replaced by much more basic thoughts, such as: When is lunch? Will I ever be clean? You're never really clean at the crematorium. A thin layer of dust and soot settles over everything, courtesy of the ashes of dead humans and industrial machinery. It settles in places you think impossible for dust to reach, like the inner lining of your nostrils. By midday I looked like the Little Match Girl, selling wares on a nineteenth-century street corner.

There is not much to enjoy in a layer of inorganic human bone dusted behind one's ear or gathered underneath a fingernail, but the ash transported me to a world different from the one I knew outside the crematorium.

Enkyo Pat O'Hara was the head of a Zen Buddhist centre in New York City at the time of the September 11 attacks, when the towers of the World Trade Center came down in a scream of chaos and metal. 'The smell didn't go away for several weeks and you had the sense you were breathing people,' she said. 'It was the smell of all kinds of things that had totally disintegrated, including people. People and electrical things and stone and glass and everything.'

The description is grisly. But O'Hara advised people not to run from the image, but instead to notice, to acknowledge that 'this is what goes on all the time but we don't see it, and now we can see it and smell it and feel it and experience it.' At Westwind, for what felt like the first time, I was seeing, smelling, feeling, experiencing. This type of encounter was an engagement with reality that was precious, and quickly becoming addictive.

Returning to my first basic concern: When, and where, was lunch? I was given half an hour for lunchtime. I couldn't eat in the lobby for fear a family would catch me feasting on chow mein. Potential scenario: front door swings open, my head jerks up, wide-eyed, noodles hanging from my lips. The crematorium was also out, lest the dust settle into my takeout container. That left the chapel (if it wasn't occupied with a body) and Joe's office.

Though Mike now ran the crematorium, Westwind Cremation & Burial was the house that Joe built. I had never met Joe (né Joaquín), the owner of Westwind: he retired just before I cremated my first body, leaving Mike in charge. He became somewhat of an apocryphal figure. Physically absent, perhaps, but still a spectre in the building. Joe had an invisible pull over Mike, watching him work, making sure he stayed busy. Mike had the same effect on me. We both worried about the iron glare of our supervisors.

Joe's office sat empty — a windowless room filled with boxes and boxes of old cremation permits, records of each person who'd made their last stop at Westwind. His picture still hung over his desk: a tall man with pockmarked skin, a scarred face, and thick black facial hair. He looked like someone you didn't want to fuck with.

After pestering Mike for more information about Joe, he produced a faded copy of a local newspaper with Joe's picture splashed across the cover. In the picture he stands in front of Westwind's cremation machines with his arms crossed and looks, once again, like someone you didn't want to fuck with.

'I found this in the filing cabinet,' Mike said. 'You'll like this. The article makes Joe sound like some badass renegade cremationist who took on the bureaucracy and won.'

Mike was right, I did like it.

'People in San Francisco eat that kind of story *up*.'

A former San Francisco police officer, Joe had founded Westwind twenty years prior to my arrival. His original business plan was to fill the lucrative niche of scattering ashes at sea. He purchased a boat and fixed it up to

25

shuttle families into the San Francisco Bay.

'I think he sailed that thing himself. From, like, China or somewhere. I don't remember,' Mike said.

Somewhere along the line, the guy storing Joe's boat made some manner of horrible mistake and sank it.

Mike explained, 'So Joe's standing there on the dock, right? Smoking a cigar and watching his boat sink into the bay. And he's thinking, well, maybe the silver lining here is that I'll use this insurance money to buy cremation machines instead.'

Fast-forward a year or so and we find Joe as the owner of a small business, the proprietor of the fledgling Westwind Cremation & Burial. He discovered that the San Francisco College of Mortuary Science had been under contract for many years with the city of San Francisco to dispose of their homeless and indigent dead.

According to Mike, 'The mortuary college's definition of 'dispose' was, like, using the bodies as learning tools for their students, unnecessarily embalming all the corpses and charging the city for it.'

In the late 1980s the mortuary college was overbilling the city by as much as $15,000 a year. So Joe, enterprising gentleman that he was, underbid the mortuary college by two dollars a body and won the contract. All the unclaimed, indigent dead now came through Westwind.

This bold move put Joe on the wrong side of the San Francisco Coroner's Office. The coroner at the time, Dr. Boyd Stephens, was chummy with local funeral homes and, according to the article, not above accepting liquor and chocolate in appreciation for his business. Dr. Stephens was equally friendly with the San Francisco College of Mortuary Science, the place Joe had just beaten for the contract to dispose of the indigent dead. Harassment against Westwind ensued, with city inspectors dropping by multiple times a week finding frivolous violations. For no reason and without warning, the city pulled the contract from Westwind. Joe filed a lawsuit (which he won) against the San Francisco Coroner's Office. Mike finished with the story with a flourish, announcing that Westwind Cremation & Burial has been *open* for business, and the San Francisco College of Mortuary Science *out* of business, ever since.

★ ★ ★

After lunch, an hour or so after sliding Mr. Martinez into the retort, it was time to move

27

him. His corpse had entered the machine feet-first, allowing the main cremation flame to shoot down from the ceiling of the chamber and hit him in the upper chest. The chest, the thickest part of the human body, takes the longest to burn. Now that his chest had had its turn with the flame, his body had to be moved forward in the chamber so that his lower half could do the same. For this I donned my industrial gloves and goggles and fetched my trusty metal pole with a flat solid rake at the end. I raised the door of the retort about eight inches, inserted the pole into the flames and carefully hooked Mr. Martinez by the ribs. The ribs were easy to miss at first, but once you got the hang of it you could usually hook the sturdiest rib on the first try. Once he was successfully hooked, I yanked him towards me in one quick movement. This pull caused a bright burst of new flames as the lower body was at last addressed with fire.

When Mr. Martinez had been reduced to red glowing embers — red is important, as black means 'uncooked' — I turned the machine off, waited until the temperature crept down to 260°C, and swept out the chamber. The rake at the end of the metal pole removes the larger chunks of bones, but a good cremationist uses a fine-toothed metal broom for hard-to-reach ashes. If you're in the right frame of mind, the bone sweeping can reach a rhythmic Zen, much like the Buddhist monks who rake sand gardens. Sweep and glide, sweep and glide.

After sweeping all of Mr. Martinez's bones into the metal bin, I carried them over to the other side of the crematorium and poured them along a long, flat tray. The tray, similar to the kind used on archaeological digs, was used to search for various metal items that people had embedded in their bodies during their lifetimes. The metal I was looking for could be anything from knee and hip implants to metal dentures.

The metal had to be removed because the final step in the cremation process was placing the bones into the waiting Cremulator. 'The Cremulator' sounds like a cartoon villain or the name of a monster truck but is in fact the name of what is essentially a bone blender, roughly the size of a slow cooker.

I swept the bone fragments from the tray into the Cremulator and set the dial to twenty seconds. With a loud whir, the bone fragments were crushed into the uniform powdery puree that the industry calls cremated remains. In California, it is assumed (and is, in fact, the law) that Mr. Martinez's family would receive fluffy white ashes in their urn, not chunks of bone. Bones would be a harsh reminder that Mr. Martinez's urn contained not just an abstract concept but an actual former human.

Not every culture prefers to avoid the bones. In the first century AD, the Romans built tall cremation pyres from pine logs. The uncoffined corpse was laid atop the pyre and set ablaze. After the cremation ended, the mourners collected the bones, hand-washed them in milk, and placed them in urns.

Lest you think bone washing hails only from the ancient bacchanalian past, bones also play a role in the death rituals of contemporary Japan. During *kotsuage* ('the gathering of the bones') the mourners gather around the cremation machine when the bones are pulled out of the chamber. The bones are laid on a table and the family members come forward with long chopsticks to pick them up and transfer them into the urn. The family first plucks the bones of the feet, working their way up towards the head, so that the deceased person can walk into eternity upright.

At Westwind there was no family: only Mr. Martinez and me. In a famous treatise called 'The Pornography of Death,' the anthropologist Geoffrey Gorer wrote, 'In many cases, it would appear, cremation is chosen because it is felt to get rid of the dead more completely and finally than does burial.' I was not Mr. Martinez's family; I did not know him, and yet there I was, the bearer of all ritual and all actions surrounding his death. I was his one-woman *kotsuage*. In times past and in cultures all over the world, the ritual following a death has been a delicate dance performed by the proper practitioners at the proper time. For me to be in charge of this man's final moments, with no training other than a few weeks operating a cremation machine, did not seem right.

After whirling Mr. Martinez to ash in the Cremulator, I poured him into a plastic bag and sealed it with a bread-bag twist tie. The plastic bag containing Mr. Martinez went into a brown plastic urn. We sold more expensive urns than this one in the arrangement room out front, gilded and decorated with mother-of-pearl doves on the side, but Mr. Martinez's family, like most families, chose not to buy one.

I punched his name into the label maker, which hummed and spat out the identity that would be stuck on the front of his eternal holding chamber. In my last act for Mr. Martinez, I placed him on a shelf above the cremation desk, where he joined the line of brown plastic soldiers, dutifully waiting for someone to come to claim them. Satisfied at having done my job and taken a man from corpse to ash, I left the crematorium at five p.m., covered in my fine layer of people dust.

The Thud

They say the way to figure out your porn-star name is to combine the name of your first childhood pet with the name of the street you grew up on. By that rule, my porn-star name would be Superfly Punalei. I have no intention of pursuing a career in pornography, but the name is almost reason enough to try.

Punalei Place is the small cul-de-sac in Kaneohe, Hawai'i, where I spent the first eighteen years of my life. My house was average at best, but due to its location on a tropical island it had the good fortune of being flanked on one side by an epic mountain range and on the other by a sparkling blue bay. You had to sprint up the front walkway during coconut season lest an overripe coconut hurl itself down onto your head.

In its languid stillness, Punalei Place was like a warm bath that never cooled. Everything would go on forever as it always had been: the pickup trucks with the feathered warrior heads hanging from their rear-view mirrors, the local plate-lunch restaurants serving teriyaki beef next to macaroni salad, ukuleles strumming their steady drone on the island music radio station. The air was thicker than it should be, and never ranged far from the same temperature as your body.

Superfly arrived from Koolau Pet Store when I was five years old, carried in a plastic bag of filtered water. He lived in my dining room in a blue tank with orange gravel. My parents named him Superfly after the title of the Curtis Mayfield hit, but it's doubtful my fish experienced the hustlin' times and ghetto streets described in the song.

Shortly after coming to live at Punalei Place, Superfly developed *Ichthyophthirius multifiliis*. Known as 'ich' or 'ick' in the aquarium trade, the parasite promises a slow aquatic death. White spots started spreading over Superfly's scales. His once-playful swimming slowed to a pathetic float. One morning, after weeks of his colour rinsing from brilliant gold to dull white, he ceased to swim at all. My mother awoke to find his tiny corpse floating in the tank. Not wanting to alarm me, she decided to put off her daughter's first mortality conversation until returning home from work that afternoon.

Later my mother sat me down, solemnly grabbing my hand. 'Sweetie, there's something I have to tell you about Superfly.'

'Yes, Mother?'

I probably called her Mom or Mommy, but

34

in my memories I'm a very polite British child with exquisite manners.

'Superfly got sick, which made him die. I saw this morning that he wasn't alive any more,' she said.

'No, Mother. That's not right,' I insisted. 'Superfly is fine.'

'Honey, I'm sorry. I wish he wasn't dead, but he is.'

'Come look, you're wrong!'

I led my mother over to Superfly's tank, where a motionless white fish floated near the surface. 'Look, Caitlin, I'm going to give him a poke, to show you what I mean, OK?' she said, lifting the top.

As she brought her finger down to touch the little carcass, Superfly shot forward, swimming across the tank to escape the jabbing human.

'Jesus Chri — !' she squealed, watching as he swam back and forth, very much alive.

This is when she heard my father laughing behind her.

'John, what did you do?' she said, clutching her chest.

What my father had done was wake up slightly later than my mother, drink his usual cup of coffee, and then unceremoniously dispose of Superfly in the toilet. He took me back to Koolau Pet Store to purchase a healthy white fish of exact Superfly dimensions. This new fish came home and plopped into the blue plastic tank, the sole purpose of its short fish life to give my mother a heart attack.

It worked. We named our new pet Superfly II and my first lesson in death was the possibility of cheating it.

Other than poor Superfly (and Superfly II, shortly thereafter), for most of my childhood I saw death only in cartoons and horror movies. I learned very early in life how to fast-forward videocassette tapes. With that skill I was able to skip the death scene of Bambi's mother, the even more traumatic death scene of Little Foot's mother in *The Land Before Time*, and the 'off with her head' scene in *Alice in Wonderland*. Nothing sneaked up on me. I was drunk with power, able to fast-forward through anything.

Then came the day that I lost my control over death. I was eight years old the evening of the Halloween costume contest at Windward Mall, only four blocks from my house. Intending to be a princess, I had found a blue sequined ball gown at a thrift store. When I realised that something as clichéd as 'princess' was not going to win me any trophies, I decided, eyes on the prize, go scary or go home.

Out of the dress-up box came a long black wig, a prop I would later use for such vital artistic projects as a cringe-inducing rendition of Alanis Morissette's 'You Oughta Know' filmed on my family's 1980s videotape camcorder. On top of the wig sat a broken tiara. The finishing touch was fake blood — a few healthy squirts sealed it. I had transformed into a D.I.Y. dead prom queen.

When my turn came at the costume contest, I limped and shuffled down the atrium runway. The master of ceremonies asked me over the mall loudspeaker who I was supposed to be, and I answered in a zombie monotone, 'He llleeefft me. Now he will paaayyy. I am the dead prom queen.' I think it was that voice that won the judges over. My prize money was $75 — enough, I calculated, for an obscene amount of Pogs. If you were a third-grader living in Hawai'i in 1993, you structured your whole life around getting enough money for Pogs.

After taking off the sequined gown in a department store bathroom, I changed into a pair of neon-green leggings under a neon pink T-shirt (also very Hawai'i in 1993) and went to the mall's haunted house with my friends. I wanted to find my father, hoping to charm him into giving me enough money for one of those giant pretzels. Like many malls, this one was two storeys, with an open floor plan that allowed people on the higher floor to look down at the action below.

I spotted my father dozing on a bench at the food court. 'Dad!' I yelled from the second storey. 'Pretzel, Dad! Pretzel!'

As I shouted and waved my arms, I saw out of the corner of my eye a little girl climb up to where the escalator met the second-storey railing. As I watched, she tipped over the edge and fell thirty feet, landing face-first on a laminate counter with a sickening thud.

'My baby! No, my baby!' shrieked her mother, barrelling down the escalator, violently shoving mall patrons aside as the crowd swarmed forward. To this day, I have never heard anything so otherworldly as that woman's screams.

My knees buckled, and I looked down to where my father had been sitting, but he was gone with the surge of the crowd. Where he had been sitting there was only an empty bench.

That thud — that noise of the girl's body hitting laminate — would repeat in my mind over and over, dull thud after dull thud. Today, the thuds might be called a symptom of post-traumatic stress disorder, but back then the noises were just the drumbeat of my childhood.

'Hey, kid, don't *you* try and jump down too — just take the escalator, OK?' my dad said, trying to be lighthearted, with the same goofy grin he had used on my mom after the Superfly incident.

I didn't think it was funny at all. I think my eyes told him nothing was funny any more.

There is a Japanese myth that tells of the descent of Izanagi into the underworld to find his sister, Izanami. When he finds her, she tells him that she will return with him to the world of the living, but — in a parallel to the Western myth of Orpheus — under no circumstances should he look at her. Izanagi is impatient, and lights a torch to see her. The torchlight reveals Izanami's corpse, rotting and covered in maggots. She attempts to chase her brother, but he draws a giant rock between them so they are separated forever. No longer ignorant of death, Izanagi must place the rock to shield him from his own thoughts, now filled with the horrors he discovered.

I sat up until dawn that night, afraid to turn out the lights. It was as if the little girl had fallen into a pit of fear in the centre of my body. There had been no violence or gore; I had seen worse on television. But this was reality. Until that night I hadn't truly understood that I was going to die, that everyone was going to die. I didn't know who else had this debilitating piece of information. If others did possess this knowledge, I wondered, how could they possibly live with it?

The next morning, my parents found me huddled on the couch in the living room under several blankets, my eyes wide. They took me for chocolate-chip pancakes at the Koa House Restaurant. We never spoke about the 'incident' again.

What is most surprising about this story is not that an eight-year-old witnessed a death, but that it took her eight whole years to do so. A child who had never seen a death would have been unheard-of only a hundred years ago.

North America is built on death. When the first European settlers arrived, all they did was die. If it wasn't starvation, the freezing cold, or battles with the Native people, it was influenza, diphtheria, dysentery, or smallpox that did them in. At the end of the first three years of the Jamestown settlement in Virginia, 440 of the original 500 settlers were dead. Children, especially, died *all the time*. If you were a mother with five children, you were lucky to have two of them live past the age of ten.

Death rates didn't improve much in the

eighteenth and nineteenth centuries. A popular chant for a children's jump-rope game went:

Grandmother, Grandmother,
Tell me the truth.
How many years
Am I going to live?
One, two, three, four . . . ?

The sad truth was that many wouldn't live longer than a few skips in the rope. During funerals, children were enlisted to act as pallbearers for other children, carrying their tiny coffins through the streets. A dismal task, but those children's long walk to the grave could be no worse than the terrors my young brain conjured after watching that little girl plunge through the air.

On a Girl Scout field trip to the local fire station a few months after the episode at the mall, I got up the nerve to ask one of the firemen what had happened to the girl. 'It was real bad,' he said, shaking his head and looking at the ground in despair.

That wasn't good enough for me. I wanted to ask, 'Real bad like they still haven't found some of her organs, or real bad like it was an incredible trauma; I can't believe she survived?'

I didn't even know whether she was alive or

dead, and I was far too terrified to ask. Very quickly it ceased to matter to me. Oprah could have brought me on her show and, her hands waving wildly, announced, 'Caitlin, you don't know it, but that girl is ALIIIIIVE and here she IIIIIS' and it wouldn't have changed the fear that had already infected me. I had started seeing death everywhere. It lived at the very edge of my peripheral vision — a fuzzy, cloaked figure that disappeared when I turned to face him head-on.

There was a student in my class, Bryce Hashimoto, who had leukemia. I didn't know what leukemia was, but a fellow classmate told me it made you throw up and die. As soon as he described the disease, I knew, at once, that it afflicted me as well. I could feel it eating me from the inside out.

Fearing death, I wanted to reclaim control over it. I figured it *had* to play favourites; I just needed to make sure I was one of those favourites.

To limit my anxiety I developed a whole bouquet of obsessive compulsive behaviours and rituals. My parents could die at any moment. *I* could die at any moment. It was my job to do everything right — counting, tapping, touching, checking — to retain balance in the universe and avoid further death.

The rules of the game were arbitrary but did not feel irrational. Walk the perimeter of my house three times in a row before feeding my dog. Step over fresh leaves; plant feet directly on dead leaves instead. Check five times to make sure the door had locked. Jump into bed from three feet away. Hold your breath when passing the mall so small children don't go plummeting off the balcony.

My elementary school principal called my parents in for a chat. 'Mr. and Mrs. Doughty, your daughter has been spitting into the front of her shirt. It's a distraction.'

For months I had been ducking my mouth down into my shirt and releasing my saliva into the fabric, letting the wet stain slowly spread downward like a second collar. The reasons for this were obscure. Somehow I had decided that failing to drool down my shirt sent a direct message to the governing powers of the universe that I didn't want my life badly enough, and that they were free to throw me to the wolves of death.

There is a treatment for obsessive compulsive disorder called cognitive-behavioural therapy. By exposing the patient to her worst fears, she can see that the disastrous outcome she expects will not occur, even if she doesn't perform her rituals. But my parents had grown up in a world where therapy was for the insane and the disturbed, not their cherished eight-year-old child (who just happened to spit into her shirt collar and obsessively tap her fingers on the kitchen counter).

As I grew older and the constant thoughts of death subsided, the rituals ended, and the thuds stopped haunting my dreams. I developed a thick layer of denial about death in order to live my life. When the feelings would come, the emotions, the grief, I would push them down deeper, furious at myself for allowing them to peek through. My inner dialogue could be ruthless: *You're fine. You're not starving, no one beats you. Your parents are still alive. There is real sadness in the world and yours is pathetic, you whiny, insignificant cow.*

Sometimes I think of how my childhood would have been different if I had been introduced directly to death. Made to sit in his presence, shake his hand. Told that he would be an intimate companion, influencing my every move and decision, whispering, 'You are food for worms' in my ear. Maybe he would have been a friend.

So, really, what was a nice girl like me doing working at a ghastly ol' crematorium like Westwind? The truth was, I saw the job as a way to fix what had happened to the eight-year-old me. The girl kept up at night by fear, crouched under the covers, believing if death couldn't see her, then he couldn't take her.

Not only could I heal myself, but I could develop ways to engage children with mortality from early on so that they didn't end up as traumatised as I was by their first experience with death. The plan was simple. Picture this: an elegant house of bereavement — sleek and modern, but with an Old World charm. It was going to be called La Belle Mort. 'Beautiful death,' in French. At least, I was fairly sure it meant beautiful death. I needed to double-check before opening my future funeral home, so I wasn't like those girls who think they're getting the Chinese character for 'hope' tattooed on their hip when in fact it is the Chinese character for 'gas station.'

La Belle Mort would be a place where families could come to mourn their dead in exciting new ways and put the 'fun' back into 'funeral.' Perhaps, I reasoned, our pathological fear of death comes from treating it as so much gloom and doom. The solution was to do away with all the nonsense of the 'traditional' funeral.

Out the door with you, expensive caskets,

tacky flower wreaths, and embalmed corpses in suits. Sayonara, canned eulogies featuring 'Lo as you walk through the valley of sad stuff,' and stacks of greeting cards with sunsets and saccharine platitudes like 'She's in a better place.'

Our traditions had held us back for far too long. It was time to get out from underneath the cloud of death denial and into celebration mode. There would be parties and merriment at La Belle Mort. It would usher in the new age of the twenty-first-century spectacle funeral. Dad's cremated ashes could be sent into space, or tamped into bullets and shot out of a gun, or turned into a wearable diamond. I would likely end up catering to celebrity types; Kanye West was sure to want a laser hologram of himself next to twelve-foot-high Champagne fountains at his memorial service.

Back in the crematorium at Westwind, as I waited for a pair of decedents to burn, I made lists of what I was going to offer at La Belle Mort Funeral Home: ashes turned into paintings, crushed into tattoo ink, made into pencils or hourglasses, shot out of a glitter cannon. My Belle Mort notebook had a simple black cover, but the front page was covered in pastel stickers of giant-eyed animals like something from a Margaret Keane painting. I thought it made the contents more upbeat, but in retrospect it probably increased the creepy factor tenfold.

'What are you always writing over here?' Mike asked, peeking over my shoulder.

'Never you mind, boss. It's just the death revolution. Never you mind,' I replied with no irony, scribbling the outline of a potential funeral package where an ash-scattering yacht carried your family out into the San Francisco Bay as a string quartet played a movement from Schubert's *Death and the Maiden*.

In my imagination, La Belle Mort appeared as the promised land of the postmodern designer funeral experience. Now that I had finally secured a real funeral job at Westwind, all I needed to do was get up every day and put on my ridiculously too-short pants and steel-toed boots and pay my dues in the trenches, burning bodies. If I worked hard enough no one could say I had never actually worked my way up through the death industry.

There were other eight-year-olds in the world, and if I could make death safe, clean, and beautiful for them, my sins would be absolved, and I too would emerge from the crematorium fires cleansed.

Toothpicks in Jell-O

Though you may never have attended a funeral, two of the world's humans die every second. Eight in the time it took you to read that sentence. Now we're at fourteen. The dead space this process out nicely so that the living hardly even notice they're undergoing the transformation. Unless a celebrity or public figure dies, we tend to overlook the necro demographic as they slip away into history.

Someone must take care of these corpses, who have become useless at caring for themselves. Someone must pick them up from homes and hospitals and transport them to the places we hide the bodies — mortuaries and coroners' offices. In Dante's *Inferno* the job fell to Charon, a shaggy-jowled, white-haired demon who piloted sinners by boat across the River Styx into hell.

At Westwind Cremation, that job belonged to Chris.

Chris was in his late fifties, tanned with a shock of white hair and sad basset-hound eyes. He was always impeccably clean and wore khakis and a button-down shirt

— California formal wear. I took to him immediately. He reminded me of Leslie Nielsen, star of the *Naked Gun* movies, which were my favourite as a child.

Chris's voice was slow and monotonous. He was a bachelor — never married, never had children. He rented a small apartment he would return to in the evening to eat a bowl of ramen and watch *Charlie Rose*. Chris was pessimistic and borderline curmudgeonly, but in a way that brought me happiness, like watching a Walter Matthau movie.

As the body-transport driver, Chris technically worked for Mike, even though he was older than his boss and had been in the funeral industry longer. Chris and Mike's conversations were akin to old-time comedy routines. Chris would walk into Mike's office and monologue in painstaking detail his planned driving route to pick up the recently deceased Mr. Kim in Berkeley, taking into account possible traffic, construction, and the evils of the modern world. Mike would grunt and half nod, elaborately ignoring him, focused on the computer screen, filing death certificates without really listening.

Picking up a person who has died at home is known as a house call. Doctors may not make them any more, but morticians are happy to come, day or night. Protocol in the

49

funeral industry says that one person may go alone to pick up bodies from hospitals, nursing homes, and the coroner's office, but a team of two people must pick up a person who died at home. When a house call came in, I was to be Chris's number two.

I appreciated the two-person rule tremendously. The gurney was the most uncooperative, unyielding machine e'er created by man. It tried, in sinister fashion, to embarrass you in front of your boss by being clunky and useless at every turn. The gurney was the only thing in this world less cooperative than the dead bodies that were strapped to them. The thought of having to operate a gurney alone in someone's private home was horrifying.

★　★　★

The first house call I went on, a week into working at Westwind, was in South San Francisco. The deceased was Mrs. Adams, an African American woman in her late forties who had died of breast cancer.

To pick up Mrs. Adams, Chris and I hopped into the van, his version of Charon's boat. This particular van, which Chris had owned for more than twenty years, was a white, windowless box of a vehicle, the kind they featured in televised public service announcements to remind children not to accept lifts from strangers. Westwind owned its own removal van — much newer, dark-blue, designed and outfitted with special features for picking up the dead. But Chris liked routine. He liked *his* van.

As we drove over the massive Bay Bridge connecting Oakland to San Francisco, I made the mistake of commenting on how beautiful the city looked that day.

Chris was horrified. 'Yeah,' he said, 'but you live there, so you know once you get up close it's just a noisy and dirty hell pit. It would be better if we just firebombed the whole city. That is — if we even make it across.'

'What do you mean *if* we make it across?' I asked, still adjusting to the concept of fire-bombing.

'Think about the way this bridge is built, Cat' — he called me Cat — 'crammed up here on eighty-foot Douglas fir pilings just stuck in the mud. It's like toothpicks in Jell-O, structurally. We're just swaying up here. The legs could just snap in half like twigs any second, and we're all dead.'

I laughed at a slightly higher pitch than usual, glancing out the window at the long drop to the Bay below.

We pulled up outside the Adamses' home twenty minutes later with none of the pomp and pageantry of the funeral carriages of old. In lieu of plumed horses in a cortège, it was Chris and me in his twenty-year-old unmarked white van.

Before we went in, I made Chris go over everything again. I wasn't about to embarrass myself in front of this woman's husband.

'Don't worry about it, Cat. A monkey could do this job. I'll talk you through it.'

As we got closer to the house, it became clear that we would not be dealing with just the woman's husband. At least fifteen people were milling around outside, eyeing us suspiciously as we walked up the front path to the door. When we walked through the front door we found ourselves in a high-ceilinged living room, where at least forty people were gathered around a woman's body. Like the scratch of a needle on a skipping record, their voices all went silent at once as the group turned to look at us.

Oh great, I thought, the only two white people here have arrived to take their beloved matriarch away in our roving child-molester van.

Chris, however, didn't miss a beat. 'Hello, folks, we're here from Westwind Cremation & Burial. Is this Mrs. Adams here?' he asked, gesturing to the dead body in the centre of the room.

It was a pretty safe bet to assume that this was, in fact, Mrs. Adams, but the group seemed to appreciate the question. A man stepped out and introduced himself as Mr. Adams.

Quick to prove myself useful, I asked in a solemn tone, 'Were you her husband?'

'Young lady, I *am* her husband. Not *were* her husband,' he replied, fixing me with a withering gaze, compounded by the forty other withering gazes from around the room.

This is it, I thought. I'm done. I have shamed myself and my family and all is lost.

However, Chris was, again, unfazed. 'Well, I'm Chris, and this is Caitlin,' he said. 'Are we ready to take her, here?'

At this point the family usually leaves the room, leaving the funeral-home employees to do whatever they do with the corpse to make it disappear. But this family wanted to watch us. This meant my first time removing a dead body from a home was going to be in front of forty crying people who hated me.

This was the moment I learned the magic of Chris. He began talking me through the process in the same voice he'd told Mike about the day's elaborate traffic route. He explained how we were going to remove Mrs. Adams as if he were telling the crowd.

'Now we're going to pull the gurney right alongside the bed, and Caitlin is going to use that handle there to lower her side down. I'm going to take the sheet next to her head and Caitlin is going to take the sheet by her feet and slide it right underneath her. Caitlin is going to pick up her feet onto the gurney in one, two, three. Now she's going to wrap the second sheet over her and snap her in tightly.'

This continued until Mrs. Adams was swathed and buckled securely to the gurney. The people in the room paid rapt attention to the process, following Chris's voice step by step. I was grateful that he didn't expose me as a fraud. I didn't even really *feel* like a fraud. The way Chris explained things made me believe I actually knew what I was doing. Surely there had never been a time I hadn't been an expert body shrouder.

As we wheeled Mrs. Adams out the front door, her son came up to us. He was my age, and his mother was dead. He wanted to lay a flower on the gurney. I didn't know what to say, so I blurted out, 'She must have been a really amazing woman. Trust me, I can just tell about these things.'

This was, of course, a lie. This was my very first house call and I still didn't know how to properly wrap the body in a sheet, forget measuring the vibe of the room to determine just how 'amazing' a dead person was when they were living.

'Um, yeah, thank you,' he said.

Driving away from the house, Mrs. Adams rattling gently in the back, Chris assured me that I hadn't actually screwed everything up forever. 'Look, Cat, we see people at their worst moments. Maybe if someone's buying a new car, or a new house, they want to be there. But what are they buying from us? Nothing, we're charging money to take *away* someone they love. That's the last thing in the world they want.' This made me feel better.

★   ★   ★

Westwind's two cremation machines could handle six bodies (three in each retort) on a typical 8:30–5:00 day — thirty souls a week during busy periods. Each removal took at least forty-five minutes, far longer if the deceased was across the bridge in San Francisco. By all rights Chris and I should have been out fetching bodies constantly. Chris *was* out constantly, but often just to avoid Mike by volunteering to run petty errands like picking up death certificates and going to the post office. I mostly stayed at Westwind and focused on cremation, since the majority of body pickups didn't require a number two. Most deaths no longer happen at home.

Dying in the sanitary environment of a hospital is a relatively new concept. In the late nineteenth century, dying at a hospital was reserved for indigents, the people who had nothing and no one. Given the choice, a person wanted to die at home in their bed, surrounded by friends and family. But times have changed, and these days, of the half a million people who die each year in the UK, only 18 per cent die in their home (although 60 per cent say they would like to, given the choice).

The 1930s brought what is known as the 'medicalisation' of death. The rise of the hospital removed from view all the gruesome sights, smells, and sounds of death. Whereas before a religious leader might preside over a dying person and guide the family in grief, now it was doctors who attended to a patient's final moments. Medicine addressed life-and-death issues, not appeals to heaven. The dying process became hygienic and heavily regulated in the hospital. Medical professionals deemed unfit for public consumption what death historian Philippe Ariès called the 'nauseating spectacle' of mortality. It became taboo to 'come into a room that smells of urine, sweat, and gangrene, and where the sheets are soiled.' The hospital was a place where the dying could undergo the indignities of death without offending the sensibilities of the living.

In my high school, my classmates and I had been told in no uncertain terms that we would not get into college and thus would never get a job and thus would end up unsuccessful and alone if we didn't serve a certain amount of summer volunteer hours. So the summer between my sophomore and junior years, I signed up to volunteer at Queen's Medical Center, a hospital in downtown Honolulu. They confirmed I was not a drug user and had decent grades, and gave me a hideous bright-yellow polo shirt and a name tag and told me to report to the volunteer office.

The volunteer department allowed you to select two areas of the hospital to rotate between from week to week. I had no interest in popular choices like the gift shop or the maternity ward. 'Get Well Soon' balloons and crying babies seemed like a cloying, sappy way to spend the summer. My first choice was working the front desk at the intensive care unit, imagining a glamorous-nurse-wiping-fevered-brows scenario out of World War II.

The ICU was not the thrill ride I had expected. Turns out, they never called the high school student in from the reception desk to assist the doctors in life-saving procedures. Instead, the job entailed hours of watching incredibly worried families wander in and out of the waiting room to use the restroom and retrieve cups of coffee.

I had more success with my second choice, the distribution department. Working for the distribution department meant passing out mail and memos to different wings of the hospital or wheeling old women out to the front kerb after they were discharged. But it also meant transferring dead bodies from wherever they had expired to the morgue in the basement. I coveted that task. The people who worked full-time in the department may not have understood my enthusiasm, but when there was a 'code black' called for a corpse transfer, they would generously wait for me to arrive.

In retrospect, it seems odd that the hospital administration would say, 'Sure thing, fifteen-year-old volunteer, you're on corpse-transfer duty.' I can't imagine this was something they normally assigned to young volunteers. In fact, I recall a fair amount of initial reluctance on their part — overcome by my successful begging.

Kaipo, my direct supervisor, a young local Hawaiian man, would look at the board and declare in his thick pidgin accent, 'Eh,

Caitlin, you like come get Mr. Yamasake from Pauahi Wing?' Oh yes, I most certainly did want to get Mr. Yamasake.

Kaipo and I arrived in Mr. Yamasake's room to find him curled up in the foetal position on his immaculate white hospital bed. He looked like a museum mummy, with taut skin like brown leather. He was less than seven stones, desiccated by disease and old age. Either one of us could have lifted him onto the stretcher with one hand.

'Dang, dis guy's pretty old, yeah?' Kaipo said, Mr. Yamasake's age surprising even a veteran of the corpse-transfer beat.

The stretcher Kaipo and I had brought with us was actually a hollowed-out metal cage. We placed Mr. Yamasake inside before covering him with a stainless-steel top, like a lid. A white sheet was draped over the whole operation. Kaipo and I left Mr. Yamasake's room pushing what appeared to be an empty stretcher.

We rolled into the elevator with regular hospital visitors holding their teddy bears and flowers, none the wiser about the secret corpse in their midst. (The next time you see two full-grown adults moving an unoccupied stretcher in a hospital, think of Mr. Yamasake.) The others got off the elevator long before we did. Kaipo, Mr. Yamasake, and I continued down to the basement.

The hospital presented itself as a positive place of healing with the latest technology and attractive Hawaiian art prints on the walls. Everything — the false stretcher, the secret morgue in the basement — was artfully designed to mask death, to distance it from the public. Death represented a failure of the medical system; it would not be permitted to upset the patients or their families.

Kaipo and Chris from Westwind were kindred spirits in a way: two men of quiet dignity who transported the husks of the recently alive. To them it was a prosaic day job, while to the average citizen theirs was a task both mystifying and disgusting.

The first few house calls for Westwind taught me that Chris was unflappable, even when removing bodies in the cramped, near-impossible conditions of San Franciscan homes. We'd walk up perilous, winding staircases, and Chris would just sigh and say, 'Better get the portable.' The portable was a portable stretcher, the kind they use to carry casualties off the field of battle. Chris and I would strap the deceased to that sucker and bring them out on their sides, their stomachs, straight up and down, over our heads — anything it took to get them out to the van.

'It's just like moving furniture,' Chris explained. 'Geometry and physics.'

Chris was equally unflappable in the face of decomposed bodies, overweight bodies, and downright bizarre bodies. By bizarre, I mean like the time we arrived at a home in the Haight District and were escorted into a cold, decrepit basement by a gentleman who had the pointed moustache and clawed hands of horror-movie actor Vincent Price. Propped up in the corner was the dead man, curled up in a ball with a single glass eye gazing up at us. 'Well, that's weird, Cat. Him winking at us? Let's go get the portable.'

The most important thing about body removal was to never give up. Trite, perhaps, but it was Chris's mantra. He told a story about a nineteen-stone body located up three flights of stairs in a hoarder house infested with cockroaches. His number-two man that day had refused to even attempt the removal, saying they would never be able to get the person out with just the two of them. 'I just lost all respect for him right then,' Chris said. 'I hate people who don't try.'

In our long trips in his van I learned more about Chris, like his single-minded obsession with the two years in the late 1970s he spent working for a tyrannical construction manager in Hawai'i. Some Google mapping showed that during his time in Hawai'i he had lived within a three-block radius of both my newly married parents and a young Barack Obama. (It was easy to construct mundane fantasy scenarios in my head where they were all at the same corner store together or crossing the street at the same stoplight.)

★   ★   ★

A few weeks after our trip to the Adamses', Chris and I took a house call in the Marina District of San Francisco at a fancy home on a busy street. We had been chatting about Hawai'i or the weather or Mike's brusqueness when we pulled up outside. 'You know what I think about, Cat?' Chris said as we grabbed our pairs of rubber gloves. 'How we're like hit men. Like the guys in *Pulp Fiction*. They're sitting there in the car talking about a sandwich, and then they go blow someone's brains out. We're just sitting here in the car chitchatting and now we're goin' in for a dead body.'

When we knocked, a dark-haired woman in her fifties opened the door. I gave her a big, sincere smile, having learned at that point that a sincere smile was more effective than faked sympathy.

'I called you hours ago!' she shrieked.

'Well, ma'am, you do know that it is rush hour and we were coming from Oakland,' Chris said in his soothing Chris voice.

'I don't care, Mom deserves the best. Mom would have wanted everything to be dignified. She was a dignified woman, this is not dignified,' she continued, still shrieking.

'I'm sorry, ma'am, we'll take good care of her,' Chris said.

We continued into a bedroom to find Mom. As we pulled out the sheet to shroud her, the woman hurled her body over her mother, wailing dramatically. 'No, Mother, no, no! I need you, Mother, don't leave me!'

This is what raw human emotion *should* look like. It had all the signs: death, loss, gut-wrenching wailing. I wanted to be moved, but I wasn't. 'Guilt,' Chris mumbled under his breath.

'What?' I whispered back.

'Guilt. I've seen this so many times. She hasn't visited her for years. Now she's here acting like she can't live without her mother. It's bullshit, Cat,' he said. And I knew he was right.

The woman finally extricated herself from mother's corpse, and we were able to get Mom wrapped up and out the door. As we rolled the gurney out onto the busy street, people stopped and stared. Dog walkers halted and yoga moms slowed their baby carriages. They gawked at us as if we were detectives or coroners, pulling a body from a violent murder scene, not two mortuary workers handling a woman in her nineties who had died quietly at home in bed.

There hadn't always been this scandal surrounding scenes of death. When the bubonic plague swept through Europe in the 1300s, bodies of the victims would lie in the street in full view of the public, sometimes for days. Eventually the death carts would collect the dead and take them to the edge of town, where trenches were dug for mass graves. A chronicler in Italy described how bodies were layered in the ground — bodies then some dirt, bodies, then some more dirt — 'just as one makes lasagne with layers of pasta and cheese.'

Today, not being forced to see corpses is a privilege of the developed world. On an average day in Varanasi, on the banks of the Ganges in India, anywhere from eighty to a hundred cremation ghats burn. After a very public cremation (sometimes performed by young children from India's untouchable caste), the bones and ashes are released into the waters of the holy river. Cremations do not come cheap; the cost of expensive wood, colourful body shrouds, and a professional cremationist adds up quickly. Families that cannot afford a cremation but want their dead loved one to go into the Ganges will place the entire body into the river by night, leaving it there to decompose. Visitors to Varanasi see bloated corpses floating by or being eaten by dogs. There are so many of these corpses in the river that the Indian government releases thousands of flesh-eating turtles to chomp away at the 'necrotic pollutants.'

The industrialised world has established systems to prevent such unsavoury encounters with the dead. At this very moment, corpses motor down highways and interstates in unmarked white vans like the one driven by Chris. Bodies crisscross the globe in the cargo holds of aeroplanes while vacationing passengers travel above. We have put the dead beneath. Not just underground, but under the tops of fake hospital stretchers, within the bellies of our aircraft, and in the recesses of our consciousness.

It is only when the systems are subverted that we even realise they are there. After Hurricane Katrina, Dr. Michael Osterholm of the Center for Infectious Disease Research and Policy was quoted in the *Washington Post* as saying, 'One of the many lessons to emerge from Hurricane Katrina is that Americans are not accustomed to seeing unattended bodies on the streets of a major city.' Understatement of the century, Doctor.

For the few minutes it took Chris and me to roll 'Mom' from her front door to the back of the van, we gave the dog walkers and yoga moms a cheap, manageable thrill. A whiff of depravity, a small taste of their own mortality.

Push the Button

CBS News, San Francisco — A man possibly in his 20s appears to have voluntarily stood on Bay Area Rapid Transit tracks before he was fatally struck by a train at a San Francisco station around noon Saturday, BART officials said.

Witnesses claimed the man 'stood in front of the train waiting for it to hit him,' BART spokesman Linton Johnson said. 'He did not make any attempt to get out of the way.'

The man was struck and dragged under the BART train at the San Francisco Civic Center Station, halting all trains at that station for nearly three hours and causing system-wide delays, according to Johnson.

Jacob was twenty-two when he climbed down onto the BART tracks and waited for the train to end his life. Twenty-two was only one year younger than I was. He didn't look like someone who had been dragged under a train. He looked like someone who had been in a two a.m. bar fight — light facial bruising, a few cuts.

'The guy we had in here last month, the one pushed under the MUNI train, *that* guy was chopped in half,' Mike said, unimpressed.

Jacob's only major damage was the absence of his left eyeball, which presumably went missing on the tracks. But if you turned his face to the right side, he looked almost normal, as if he could open his remaining eye and hold a conversation.

The Romanian philosopher Emil Cioran said that suicide is the only right a person truly has. Life can become unbearable in all respects, and 'this world can take everything from us . . . but no one has the power to keep us from wiping ourselves out.' Perhaps not surprisingly, Cioran, a man 'obsessed with the worst,' died an insomniac and recluse in Paris.

Cioran may have been predisposed to Negative Nancyism, but madness and despair can touch us no matter our philosophies. Nietzsche, who famously said in *Twilight of the Idols*, 'What does not kill me makes me stronger,' suffered a mental breakdown at age forty-four. Eventually he fell into the full-time care of his sister, whose own husband had committed suicide in Paraguay.

Cruel and selfish as many view suicide to be, I suppose I felt supportive of Jacob's decision. If every day of his life was dull misery, I could not demand he stay alive and endure more dull misery. I couldn't know if it had been mental illness or a sense of endless despondency that had driven Jacob to suicide. It wasn't my place to speculate on his motives. But I could pass judgement on his methods. There, I was firmly not on his side.

There was something in the *way* Jacob had killed himself that unsettled me. The public spectacle of staring down a crowded train. In college, I managed a coffee shop on the University of Chicago campus. Only two months before I started at Westwind, my former assistant manager hanged himself in his bedroom after a fight with his girlfriend. His roommate had to come home to find his body. The fact that he left those two women with the lifelong burden of his suicide made me ill, even more so than his death. If you are going to take yourself out of commission, it seems only fair you do so in a way that does the least harm to others, slipping out the back door of the party of life, ensuring the other guests don't have to agonise about your choice.

Most of the damage Jacob caused by stepping in front of a BART train that day was financial: thousands of people late for work, flights from San Francisco and Oakland Airports missed, important appointments broken.

But for the train conductor, the person who had to look into Jacob's eyes as he barreled towards him, helpless to stop the train in time, the damage was not financial. The average train conductor will involuntarily kill three people in his career. Having no choice but to kill someone (or several someones) has to be the quickest way to lose affection for an otherwise stable, even desirable, job.

Nor was the damage financial for the people waiting on the platform. They had to stand there screaming for him to get out of the way: didn't he see there was a train coming? Then came the moment when they realised he knew perfectly well the train was coming, and they would be forced to witness what came next. Forced to live with the image, the sounds, their own confused screams for the rest of their lives.

Mike pointed out that a few of those people would envy the opportunity I had to cremate Jacob. 'Maybe they'd smack him around a little first,' he said. 'Some light revenge.'

As it was, they would never see his body.

Jacob would maintain his power over them, haunting their dreams.

I thought of the years I had spent reliving the little girl hitting the ground at the mall, and I felt a searing sympathy for those people. I wanted to throw open the crematorium doors to the train conductor and the other commuters. I wanted them with me that day, gathered around Jacob's body so I could announce, 'Look, here he is; he wanted to die. He is dead, but you're not. *You are not dead.*'

It was illegal, this open-house-at-the-mortuary fantasy of mine. The California Code of Regulations clearly states that 'the care and preparation for burial or other disposition of all human remains shall be strictly private.'

In the late 1800s, the citizens of Paris would come to the morgue by the *thousands* each day to view the bodies of the unidentified dead. Spectators lined up for hours to get in as vendors sold them fruit, pastries, and toys. When they reached the front of the line, they would be ushered into an exhibit room, where the corpses were laid out on slabs behind a large glass window. Vanessa R. Schwartz, scholar of fin-de-siècle Paris, called the Paris morgue 'a spectacle of the real.'

Eventually the morgue exhibitions became *too* popular with the citizens of Paris, and they were shut down to the public. Morgues remain behind closed doors today, perhaps because those in charge of regulating death believe the hoi polloi would be too interested, and that such an interest is inherently wrong. Close the morgues if you will, but another attraction will always arise to fill void. The runaway popularity of *Body Worlds*, Gunther von Hagens's travelling exhibit of plastinated human bodies, shows us that the human urge to file past corpses on display is indeed as strong as ever. In spite of the ongoing controversy that von Hagens obtained some of his bodies from Chinese political prisoners, *Body Worlds* is the most popular touring attraction in the world (having drawn 38 million people by the start of 2014).

*   *   *

Jacob lived in Washington State, and visited San Francisco for reasons unknown. His parents arranged his cremation over the phone, faxing Westwind the required forms and reading us their credit card number to cover the balance. As usual, it was just Jacob and me as I loaded him into the cremation machine, his one eye gazing up at me.

Because of his violent death, Jacob was taken to the Medical Examiner's Office before being brought to Westwind. The Medical Examiner's Office is the modernised version of the Coroner's Office, and is run by medical doctors trained to investigate suspicious or violent deaths. Whenever Westwind Cremation went to pick up a body, the examiner's staff would give us whatever personal items arrived with the deceased. This usually meant clothes, jewellery, wallets, and so on.

Jacob came with a backpack. His parents didn't want it mailed back to Washington, so the only place for it to go was into the flames alongside Jacob.

I set the backpack on a table and pulled open the zipper. Jackpot, I thought, one serving of understanding of the mind of a depressed madman, coming right up. But each item I pulled out was more obscenely normal than the next. Change of clothes, toiletries, a kombucha bottle. Then: a stack of notecards. At last! The scribblings of a suicidal lunatic? No. Chinese language flashcards.

I was disappointed. I had expected answers in that backpack, insight into the human condition.

'Hey, Caitlin, put this wallet back in there

before you cremate it,' Mike called from his office.

'Wait, there's a wallet?' I replied.

'I'm looking at his ID right now. There's his college ID, his driver's licence, his Greyhound bus ticket to San Francisco. Oh, and a map of the BART train system; that's depressing. He wrote something on the BART map. Word of the day: 'anthropophagy.' What does that mean?'

'I have no idea. I'm going to Google it right now. Spell it,' I said.

'A-N-T-H-R-O-P-O-P-H-A-G-Y.'

'Shit. It means cannibalism. It's a synonym for cannibalism,' I said.

Mike laughed at the gallows humour of the definition. 'No way. Do you think this means he had an insatiable desire for human flesh? This bus ticket says he got in to San Francisco the day before he died. Why not commit suicide back in Washington?'

'Right,' I added, 'why would you come all the way to San Francisco to stand in front of a BART train?'

'Maybe he wasn't trying to die. Just be an ass and dodge the train or something. Like that kid in *Stand by Me*.'

'Corey Feldman?' I asked.

'No, the other one.'

'River Phoenix?'

'No, not that one either,' Mike said. 'Whatever, if that's what he was trying, shit, he didn't do a very good job.'

As I slid Jacob into the flames, the only things I knew about him were that he was a twenty-two-year-old from Washington who studied Chinese and was perhaps, at least on the day he died, interested in cannibalism. A few weeks earlier I had invested my first pay cheque in the box set of the HBO television series *Six Feet Under*, the beloved show about a family-run mortuary. In one episode, Nate the funeral director visits a lonely, dying young man to arrange his cremation. The man is angry and bitter about his impending death and the lack of support from his family. He asks Nate who will push the button on the cremation machine when he dies.

'Whomever you specify,' Nate replies. 'Buddhists have a family member, and then some people choose no one, in which case the person at the crematorium does it.'

'I'll take that guy.'

That was me. The person at the crematorium. I was 'that guy' for Jacob. In spite of what he had done, I didn't want him to be alone.

★ ★ ★

75

The great triumph (or horrible tragedy, depending on how you look at it) of being human is that our brains have evolved over hundreds of thousands of years to understand our mortality. We are, sadly, self-aware creatures. Even if we move through the day finding creative ways to deny our mortality, no matter how powerful, loved, or special we may feel, we know we are ultimately doomed to death and decay. This is a mental burden shared by precious few other species on Earth.

Say you are a gazelle, grazing an African plain. The soundtrack from *The Lion King* plays in the background. A hungry lion stalks you from a distance. He sprints in to attack, but today you manage to outrun him. By instinct, a fight-or-flight reaction, you feel momentary anxiety. Experience and genetics have taught you to run and evade danger, and it does take some time for your heart to stop racing. But soon enough you can return to happy grazing as if nothing had happened. Chomp-chomp, blissful chomps, until the lion comes back for round two.

The human heart rate may decelerate after the lion chase has ended, but we *never* stop knowing that the game is lost. We know death awaits us, and it affects everything we do, including the impulse to take elaborate care of our dead.

Some 95,000 years ago, a group of early *Homo sapiens* buried their bodies in a rocky shelter known as Qafzeh Cave, located in what is now Israel. When archaeologists excavated the cave in 1934, they found that the bodies were not just buried: they were buried with purpose. Some of the surviving skeletal remains found at Qafzeh show stains of red ochre, a naturally tinted clay. Archaeologists believe the ochre's presence means that we performed rituals with our dead very early in our species' history. One of the recovered skeletons, a thirteen-year-old child, was buried with its legs bent to the side and a pair of deer antlers in its arms. We cannot understand what these ancient people thought about death, the afterlife, or the corpse, but these clues tell us they *did* think about it.

When families came to Westwind to arrange for cremations and burials, they sat in our front arrangement room and nervously drank water out of paper cups, unhappy about the death that brought them there and often even more unhappy about having to pay for it. Sometimes they'd request a viewing in our chapel in order to see the dead body for a final time. Occasionally the chapel was filled with a hundred people weeping over the strains of gospel music; other days it was just a single mourner, sitting quietly for half an hour before seeing themselves out.

Families would go through the chapel or arrangement room, even the front office, but the crematorium itself was my space. Most days I was alone 'in the back,' as Mike called it.

On our price list we offered something called a 'Witness Cremation,' but no one took us up on this offer the first few weeks I was at Westwind. Then, one day, there was the Huang family. When I showed up to work at eight thirty there were already a dozen older Asian women, in the supply cupboard of all places, setting up a makeshift altar.

'Mike?' I called out, walking towards his office.

'What's up?' he called back with his usual deadpan indifference.

'Hey, why are there people in the supply cupboard?' I asked.

'Oh, right, they're here for the witness this afternoon. There's not going to be enough room in the chapel for all their stuff, so I gave them the cupboard for the altar,' he said.

'I — I didn't know there was going to be a witness,' I fumbled, terrified at the invasion of my space and routine.

'I thought Chris told you, man. Don't worry about it, I got this one,' he said.

Mike had no qualms about the day's events. Maybe he could perform a witness cremation with one hand tied behind his back, but the whole premise seemed incalculably dangerous to me. A witness cremation followed a sequence: the family was given time in the chapel with the deceased, the body was wheeled into the crematorium, and the cremation process was begun with the whole family standing right there. *With the whole family standing right there.* About as much room for error as in the transport of nuclear weapons.

When Western cremation evolved from open pyres to enclosed industrial machines, the first of these new machines were built with peepholes in the side so the family could peek in and watch the process like a naughty show. Some funeral homes even *required* that family members be there to witness the body being loaded into the machine. But as time went on the peepholes were covered and sealed, the families kept out of the crematorium altogether.

Over the last few decades the funeral industry has evolved a number of methods to distance the family from any aspect of death that might potentially offend them, and not just in the crematorium.

When my friend Mara's grandmother

suffered a fatal stroke, Mara was on the next flight to Florida to hold vigil at the deathbed. Over the next week, Mara watched her grandmother struggle to breathe, unable to swallow or move or make a sound. When death mercifully took the old woman, Mara expected she would be there through the whole funeral as well. She wasn't. I received this message from her: 'Caitlin, we just stood there next to the open grave. Her casket was there and the dirt was covered up with Astroturf. I kept thinking they were going to lower the casket into the grave. They never did. We had to walk away while the casket was still sitting there, unburied.'

Only after Mara's family had left the cemetery would Grandmother's casket be lowered into the ground and the yellow construction diggers brought in to dump the dirt back on top.

These modern denial strategies help focus mourners on positive 'celebrations of life' — life being far more marketable than death. One of the largest funeral-home corporations keeps small toaster ovens near their arrangement rooms so fresh-baked cookie smells will comfort and distract families throughout the day — fingers crossed that the chocolate chips mask the olfactory undertones of chemicals and decomposition.

I passed back through Westwind's supply cupboard, nodding at the women who were making remarkable progress on the altar. They worked to arrange multiple bowls of fruit and circular flower wreaths at the base of a large framed picture of the deceased Mr. Huang, the patriarch of the family. The picture was in the style of a shopping-mall portrait, the head and shoulders of an older Chinese man in a sharp suit and abnormally rosy cheeks. Airbrushed clouds floated in the background.

On Mike's instructions, Chris and I brought Mr. Huang's wooden casket into the chapel. When we opened the lid, Mr. Huang was waiting for us in his best suit. He had the stiff, waxy appearance of an embalmed corpse, no longer the stern dreamer in his cloud portrait.

Throughout the morning, more and more of Mr. Huang's family arrived, bearing more fruits and gifts for the cupboard altar. 'You,' an older woman barked at me with disapproval, 'why you wear red?'

The colour red, associated with happiness, is poor form at a Chinese funeral. The cherry-red dress I wore all but screamed, 'Ha, grievers! I laugh in the face of cultural sensitivity!'

I wanted to protest that I didn't know the

Huang family would be there that day, especially for something as terrifying as a witness cremation. Instead I mumbled an apology and shuffled away with her bowl of oranges.

Mike had already gone into the back to preheat one of the retorts. When the time came for Mr. Huang's cremation, he had me follow him into the chapel. We threaded our way through throngs of Mr. Huang's relatives, clucking with displeasure at my red dress. The casket was rolled out of the chapel and into the crematorium. The family streamed in behind us, thirty people at least, invading what until now had been my sacred space.

As we filed into the crematorium, everyone (elderly women included) fell to their knees on the ground, wailing. The howls of the mourners mixed in with the roar of the cremation machine. The effect was eerie. I stood at the back, my eyes wide, feeling like an anthropologist privy to some unknown rite.

It is a Chinese practice to hire professional mourners for a ceremony to help facilitate grief, to whip the crowd into a frenzy. It was difficult to tell if some of the people on the crematorium floor were such professional mourners, hired by the family to promote sorrow through their excess emotion. Were professional mourners even available in Oakland? Their grief appeared genuine. But then again, I had never been in a situation like this before, where such a large group of people allowed themselves to be emotionally vulnerable. No stiff upper lips here.

Suddenly, a man I had somehow missed began weaving his way through the crowd with a video camera, filming the mourners. He would stop in front of a wailer and wave his hands upward, indicating what he wanted from them was *more*, more wailing! The mourner would let out a louder, more anguished cry and beat the ground. It seemed that no one wanted to get caught on camera looking calm or stoic.

The Huang family was engaged in ritual in the classic sense, mixing belief with tactile, physical action. Andrew Newberg and Eugene D'Aquili, two researchers of the human brain from the University of Pennsylvania, explained that for a ritual to work, the participants must engage 'all parts of the brain and body, it must merge behaviour with ideas.' Through their wailing, their kneeling, their grief, Mr. Huang's family were connecting to something greater than themselves.

Mr. Huang's casket slid into the cremation chamber and Mike gestured at Mr. Huang's son to push the button to start the flames. It was a symbolic gesture, but one of incredible power.

Mike said to me later, 'You *gotta* let 'em push the button, man. They love the button.'

Mr. Huang got something crucial that Jacob did not: someone he loved, not the random crematorium operator in her culturally insensitive dress, to push the button that would take him out of this world.

As the door closed, locking Mr. Huang into the fiery chamber, Chris swooped in to set a large burning candle in front of the machine. Mike and Chris had done this part as a team before. The Huangs had wailed in grief before. I was the only one who was out of place.

Mr. Huang forced me to think about what I would do if my own father died. Frankly, I hadn't a clue. There was a good chance that not everyone taking part in this witness cremation felt quite the intensity of grief they were displaying. For some it may have been more performance than genuine sorrow. But that didn't matter; the Huang family had ritual. They knew what to do and I envied them for it. They knew how to cry louder, mourn harder, and show up with bowls of fruit. At the time of death, they were a community, rallied around ideas and customs.

My father taught history at a public high school for more than forty years. Even though the school where he taught was on the other side of the island, he would wake up at five thirty every morning to drive me an hour to my private school in Honolulu, and then another hour to his own school. All so I wouldn't have to take the city bus. He had carried me for thousands of miles — how could I just hand him off to another person when he died?

As I gained more experience in the crematorium I no longer dreamt of the gracious cover-ups of La Belle Mort Funeral Home. I began to realise that our relationship with death was fundamentally flawed. After only a few months at Westwind I felt naïve for having ever imagined putting the 'fun' back in funerals. Holding 'celebration of life' ceremonies with no dead body present or even realistic talk of death, just Dad's favourite old rock-'n'-roll songs playing while everyone drank punch, seemed akin to putting not just any Band-Aid over a gunshot wound, but a Hello Kitty one. As a culture it was time to go after the bullet.

No, when my father died he would go to a crematorium. Not a warehouse like Westwind, but a beautiful crematorium with huge windows that let in gobs of natural light. But it would not be beautiful because death was hidden or denied; it would be beautiful because death would be embraced. It would be a place of experience, with rooms for families to come and wash their dead. Where they could feel safe and comfortable being with a body until its final moment, inserted into the flames.

In 1913, George Bernard Shaw described witnessing the cremation of his mother. Her body was placed in a violet coffin and loaded feet-first into the flames. 'And behold!' he wrote. 'The feet burst miraculously into streaming ribbons of garnet coloured lovely flame, smokeless and eager, like Pentecostal tongues, and as the whole coffin passed in it sprang into flame all over; and my mother became that beautiful fire.'

I pictured my father, the door of the cremation chamber rising and the reverberation filling the room. If I was still alive when he died, I would be there to watch him become 'that beautiful fire.' I didn't want anyone else to do it. The more I learned about death and the death industry, the more the thought of anyone else taking care of my own family's corpses terrified me.

Pink Cocktail

Once upon a forgotten time, the Wari' people lived in the jungles of western Brazil with virtually no contact with Western civilisation. Then, in the early 1960s, the Brazilian government arrived in Wari' territory alongside evangelical Christian missionaries, both groups trying to establish relations. The outsiders brought with them a host of diseases (malaria, influenza, measles) that the Wari' immune system had no precedent for fighting. In the span of a few years, three out of every five Wari' were dead. Those who survived became dependent on the Brazilian government, who supplied them with Western medicine to fight the new Western diseases.

In order to receive medicine, food, and government aid, the Wari' were forced to give up an important aspect of their lives — their cannibalism.

The Renaissance philosopher Michel de Montaigne wrote in his conveniently titled *Of Cannibals* that 'each man calls barbarism whatever is not his own practice.' We certainly *would* call cannibalism barbaric, and it is *not* our practice, thank you very much. Consuming human flesh is for sociopaths and savages; it conjures up images of head-hunters and Hannibal Lecter.

We can be confident that cannibalism is for the deranged and heartless because we are caught in what anthropologist Clifford Geertz called 'webs of significance.' From the time we are born, we are indoctrinated by our specific culture as to the ways death is 'done' and what constitutes 'proper' and 'respectable.'

Our biases in this matter are inescapable. As much as we fancy ourselves open-minded, we are still imprisoned by our cultural beliefs. It is like trying to walk through a forest after the spiders have been up all night spinning webs between the trees. You may be able to see your destination in the distance, but if you attempt to walk towards that destination, the spiderwebs will catch you, sticking to your face and lodging themselves awkwardly in your mouth. These are the webs of significance that make it so hard for Westerners to understand the cannibalism of the Wari'.

The Wari' were mortuary cannibals, meaning their form of cannibalism was a ritual performed at the time of death. From the moment a member of the Wari' took their last breath, their corpse was never left alone. The family rocked and cradled the body to the sound of a steady, high-pitched chant. This chanting and wailing announced the death to the rest of the community, and soon everyone joined in the hypnotic sound. Relatives from other villages rushed to get to the corpse's side to participate in the ritual for the dead.

To prepare for the consumption of the flesh, relatives walked through the village and pulled a wooden beam from every house, leaving the roofs sagging. Anthropologist Beth Conklin described this sagging as a visual reminder that death had violated the community. The wood gathered from the homes was bundled together, decorated with feathers, and used as kindling for a roasting rack.

At last the family relinquished the corpse and the body was cut into pieces. The internal organs were wrapped in leaves and the flesh from the limbs placed directly on the rack to cook. The women of the village prepared corn bread, considered an ideal pairing for human meat.

The act of cooking human flesh as if it were 'no more than a piece of meat' did not trouble the Wari'. Animals and their flesh meant (and still mean) something very different to members of the Wari' tribe than they do to us. To the Wari', animals have dynamic spirits. Animals do not belong to, nor are they any lower than, human beings. Depending on the day, humans and animals alternate between hunter and hunted. Jaguars, monkeys, and tapirs might see themselves as humans and see humans as animals. Wari' have respect for all the meat they consume, human or animal.

The people who actually consumed the roasted flesh were not the dead person's closest blood relatives, such as wives or children. That honour — and it was indeed an honour — went to chosen people who were *like* blood to the deceased: in-laws, extended relatives, and community members, known as affines. None of the affines were vengeful, flesh-hungry savages, desperate for the taste of grilled human, and neither were they after the protein the human flesh provided — both common motives ascribed to cannibals. In fact, the corpse, which had been laid out over several days in the warm, humid climate of the Amazon rain forest, was often well into various stages of decomposition. Eating the flesh would have been a smelly, foul experience. The affines often had to excuse themselves to vomit before returning to eat again. Yet they forced themselves to continue, so strong was their conviction that they were performing a compassionate act for both the family and the person who had died.

The affines weren't eating the dead to preserve life force or power; they ate to destroy.
The Wari' were horrified by the thought of a
dead body being buried and left fully intact
in the ground. Only cannibalism could provide the true fragmentation and destruction
they desired. After the flesh was consumed,
the bones were cremated. This total disappear-
ance of the body was a great comfort to the
family and community.

The dead had to be removed to make the
community whole again. The body destroyed,
the dead person's possessions, including the
crops they had planted and the home they
had built, were burned as well. With
everything gone, the family of the dead
person was at the mercy of their relatives and
community to take care of them and help
them rebuild. And the community *did* take
care of them, reinforcing and strengthening
their communal bonds.

In the 1960s the Brazilian government
forced the Wari' to give up their rituals and
begin burying their dead. Placing their dead
in the ground to rot was the absolute
opposite of what they had practised and
believed. As long as the physical body
remained intact, it was a tortuous reminder of
what had been lost.

If we had been born into the Wari' tribe,

the cannibalism we dismiss as barbarism would have been our own cherished custom, one we engaged in with sincerity and conviction. The burial practice in North America — embalming (long-term preservation of the corpse), followed by burial in a heavy sealed casket in the ground — is offensive and foreign to the Wari'. The 'truth and dignity' of the Western style of burial is only the truth and dignity as determined by our immediate surroundings.

When I began working at Westwind, modern embalming wasn't something I could clearly define. I knew it was what was 'done' with bodies, one thread in my own web of significance. When I was ten years old, my cousin's husband's father died. Mr. Aquino was a good Catholic, the elder statesman of an enormous Hawaiian-Filipino family. His funeral was held at an old cathedral in Kapolei. When we arrived, my mother and I joined the line to file past his casket. As we reached the front of the line, I peered over the edge and saw Papa Aquino laid out. He was so made up that he no longer looked real. His grey skin was stretched tight, a by-product of the embalming fluid pumped through his circulatory system. Hundreds of candles burned around his casket, and the light from their flames reflected off his shiny, bright-pink lips, contorted into a grimace. He was a dignified man in life but looked like a waxen replica of himself in death. Though the whole rigmarole of the embalmed viewing never quite took off in the same way in the UK, it was an experience I share with thousands upon thousands of other American children, trundling past a casket and getting this brief, waxy vision of death.

As to the type of person who would choose a career performing this dismal process, I vaguely imagined a gaunt man with hollowed cheeks, tall and thin like Lurch from the *Addams Family*. I crossed this vision of Lurch with the archetypal undertaker from a 1950s horror movie, wearing a lab coat and watching neon-green liquid slide through tubes into a dead body.

The embalmer at Westwind Cremation couldn't have been further from this image. Bruce, the trade embalmer who came in several times a week to prepare bodies, was an African American man with greying hair and a boyish face — positively cherubic. He looked like a six-foot-tall Gary Coleman, fifty going on twenty. His voice fluctuated wildly in pitch and rhythm and carried across the crematorium. 'Hey there, Caitlin!' he greeted me with enthusiasm.

'Hey, Bruce, how you doing?'

'You know how it is, girl, just another day. Just another day with the dead.'

Technically I was training to be a crematorium operator under Mike, but Bruce had been the assistant embalming instructor at the San Francisco College of Mortuary Science, the embalming school that closed its doors not long after Westwind underbid them on the homeless-and-indigent-dead contract. Although there was no longer a mortuary school in San Francisco, Bruce still had the instructor in him and was eager to share the secrets of the trade. Not that he had *all* that much respect for mortuary schools these days.

'Caitlin, when you learned this stuff in the old days it was an art,' he said. 'Embalming meant preserving the body. I'm telling you, I'm beginning to wonder what they actually *teach* people at these mortuary colleges. Students come out of there who can't even find a vein for drainage. Back in the '70s, you worked on the bodies every day. Everything you did was bodies — bodies, bodies, bodies, bodies.'

There is a narrative, created mostly by the North American funeral industry, that situates modern embalming practices within an age-old tradition, an art form passed down through the millennia from the ancient

94

Egyptians, original masters of corpse preservation. The present-day funeral director acts as the bearer of their ancient wisdom.

Needless to say, that narrative has a number of problems. Embalmers may claim their trade descended from the ancient Egyptians, but that neglects the quantum gap between the era of Tutankhamun and the time Americans began to perform embalmings in the early 1860s.

The embalming practised by the ancient Egyptians was a *very* different animal from what is practised down the street in your local funeral home. Some 2,500 years ago, bodies of the Egyptian elite were treated to an elaborate post-mortem process that took months to complete. In contrast, the embalming at your funeral home takes three to four hours from start to finish. That is, if you're lucky enough to get three to four hours of an embalmer's time. Large funeral corporations have been buying up mom-and-pop mortuaries for years, keeping the mom-and-pop name the community trusts, but upping their prices and centralising their embalming facilities. This gives body preparation the atmosphere of an assembly line, with embalmers pressured to knock out a completed corpse in record time.

The Egyptians embalmed for religious

reasons, believing that every step of their process — from removing the brain through the nose with a long iron hook to placing the internal organs in animal-head vases called Canopic jars to drying the body out for forty days with natron salt — had profound significance. There are no brain hooks or organ-storage jars in modern North American embalming, which instead involves the removal of blood and fluids from the body cavity and replacing them with a mixture of strong preservative chemicals. More important, modern embalming was born not from religion but from stronger forces altogether — marketing and consumerism.

On this particular day, lying on Bruce's embalming table was a man of vastly different social station from the privileged citizens once embalmed by the Egyptians. His name was Cliff, a Vietnam War veteran who had died alone at the Veterans' Administration (VA) Hospital in San Francisco. The US government pays for the embalming and burial (at a national cemetery) of veterans like Cliff — the men, and occasionally women, who die with no friends or family.

Bruce approached with a scalpel, bringing it down at the base of Cliff's throat. 'All right, now, first thing you have to do is get the blood out. Flush the system. Like flushing a radiator system in a car.'

Bruce made an incision. I was expecting blood to come gushing out like in a slasher film, but the wound was dry. 'This guy isn't exactly fresh; the VA keeps bodies for a long time,' Bruce explained, shaking his head in frustration.

Bruce showed me how to mix the salmon-pink cocktail that would replace Cliff's blood: a blend of formaldehyde and alcohol splashed into a large glass tank. Bruce stuck his gloved fingers into the new hole in Cliff's throat and sliced open the carotid artery, then inserted a small metal tube. The small tube connected to an even larger rubber tube. Bruce flipped a switch at the base of the tank and it began to vibrate and hum as the pink liquid burst through the tube, sending chemicals shooting through Cliff's circulatory system. As the liquid flowed into his artery, the displaced blood spurted forth from Cliff's jugular vein and slid down the table to the sink's drain.

'Isn't it dangerous, the blood just going down the drain like that?' I asked.

'Naw, it ain't dangerous. You know what else goes in the sewer?' Bruce said. I had to admit, this made the blood less disgusting by comparison.

'That isn't even that much blood, Caitlin,'

he continued. 'You should see when I embalm a case that's been autopsied. You get *covered* in blood, and it's not all nice and neat like on TV. It's like with OJ.'

'Wait, like OJ Simpson? How is this like OJ?'

'Now, I'm a mortician right? Sometimes when I cut up people I get *covered* in blood. You get one of those arteries where blood is shootin' out everywhere — well, you know how blood is. They said OJ cut up two people while they were still alive and walked out of there but there were only three drops of blood on the car?'

'OK, Bruce, but didn't somebody have to kill them?' I asked.

'Whoever did that business had to be wearing a body suit from head to toe. When you get soaked with blood, that stuff don't just wash off; it stains. Did you see the crime scene on CNN? That scene was a bloody mess. All I'm saying is there should have been a blood trail.'

While Bruce acted as forensic detective, he was, at the same time, gently soaping and massaging Cliff's limbs to disperse the chemicals through his vascular system. It was a bizarre image, a grown man giving a corpse a sponge bath, but by now I had grown accustomed to Westwind's peculiar tableaux.

The tilt in the porcelain embalming table helped Cliff's blood slide down into the drain as the formaldehyde solution diffused through his body. Formaldehyde, a colourless gas in its pure form, has been classified as a carcinogen. Cliff the corpse was long past caring about cancer, but Bruce was a sitting duck if he didn't take proper precautions. The National Cancer Institute has found that funeral embalmers are at an increased risk for myeloid leukemia, abnormal growth in the bone-marrow tissue, and cancer of the blood. The irony is that embalmers make a living draining the blood of others, only to have their own blood mutiny against them.

What was happening to Cliff, this chemical preservation of the corpse, had no place in American death customs prior to the Civil War in the mid-nineteenth century. Death in America began as an entirely home-grown operation. A person would die in their own bed, surrounded by their family and friends. The corpse would be washed and shrouded by the man or woman's closest living relations and laid out for several days in the home for a wake — a ritual named for the Old English word for 'keeping watch,' not, as it is often believed, the fear that the corpse might suddenly wake up.

To prevent decomposition while the body

remained at home, innovations like vinegar-soaked cloths and tubs of ice beneath the corpse were developed in the nineteenth century. During the wake there was food to be consumed, alcohol to be imbibed, and a sense of releasing the dead person from their place in the community. As Gary Laderman, scholar of American death traditions, put it, 'Although the body had lost the spark that animated it, deeply rooted social conventions demanded that it be given proper respect and care from the living.'

During the wake, a wooden coffin was constructed either by the family or perhaps a local cabinetmaker. The hexagonal coffin was tapered at the bottom, indicating this was indeed a container for a dead human, unlike today's rebrand of both the shape (a plain rectangle) and the name (casket). After several days had passed, the corpse was placed in the coffin and carried on the shoulders of family members to a nearby grave.

By the mid-nineteenth century bigger, industrial cities like New York, Baltimore, Philadelphia, and Boston became large enough to support death industries. Unlike farms or small towns, large cities maintained specialised trades. Undertaking emerged as a profession, though the job entailed little more than selling funeral props and decorations. The local undertaker might build you a coffin, rent you a hearse or funeral carriage, or sell you mourning clothes or jewellery. They often took other jobs to supplement their income, leading to some amusing nineteenth-century ads: 'John Jensen: Undertaker, Tooth Puller, Lamp Lighter, Frame Builder, Blacksmith, Cabinetmaker.'

Then came the Civil War, the deadliest war in American history. The Battle of Antietam on September 17, 1862, holds the dubious honour of having been the Civil War's (and American history's) single bloodiest day, during which 23,000 men died on the battlefield, their maggot-ridden corpses bloated amidst the equally bloated bodies of horses and mules. When the 137th Pennsylvania Regiment arrived four days later, its leader requested that his men be allowed to consume liquor as they buried the bodies, there being only one state in which it was possible to do the job: drunk.

During the four years of battles between the North and South, many of the soldiers' families had no way to retrieve their dead sons and husbands from the battlefields. The corpses could be transported on trains, but after a few days in the Southern summer heat, the dead entered the deepest throes of decomposition. The smell emanating from a body left in the sun would have been far worse than a mere olfactory inconvenience.

According to the account of a doctor for the Union army, 'during the battle of Vicksburg the two sides called for a brief armistice because of the stench of corpses disintegrating in the hot sun.' Transporting bodies hundreds of miles in this odious condition was a nightmare for train conductors, even the most patriotic among them. Railroads began refusing to transport bodies not sealed in expensive iron coffins — not a viable option for most families.

The situation brought out the entrepreneurial impulses of men, who, if a family could pay, would perform a new preservative procedure called embalming — right there on the battlefield. They followed the skirmishes and battles looking for work, America's first ambulance chasers. Competition was fierce, with stories of embalmers burning down one another's tents and placing advertisements in local papers reading, 'Bodies Embalmed by Us NEVER TURN BLACK.' To market the effectiveness of their services, the embalmers would display real preserved bodies they had plucked from the unknown dead, propping the corpses up on their feet outside the tents to better demonstrate their talents.

The embalming tents on the battlefield

often contained only a simple plank of wood atop two barrels. The embalmers injected chemicals into the arterial systems of the newly dead, their own special blends of 'arsenicals, zinc chloride, bichloride of mercury, salts of alumina, sugar of lead, and a host of salts, alkalies, and acids.' Dr. Thomas Holmes, still regarded by many in the funeral industry as the patron saint of embalming, maintained that during the Civil War he personally embalmed more than 4,000 dead soldiers in this fashion, at the cost of $100 a body. The discount option, for those not inclined towards the highbrow methods of chemicals and injections, might be to eviscerate the internal organs and fill the body cavity with sawdust. Defiling the body in this way was considered a sin in both the Protestant and Catholic traditions, but the desire to see the face of a loved one again sometimes trumped religious ideology.

The full evisceration of the body cavity is not so different from what is done today, minus the sawdust. Perhaps the dirtiest secret about the process of modern embalming is the occult use of a skinny, lightsaber-sized piece of metal known as the trocar. Bruce raised his trocar like the sword Excalibur and pushed its pointed tip into Cliff's stomach, stabbing him just below his belly button. He jabbed the trocar in, breaking the skin, and went to work puncturing Cliff's intestines, bladder, lungs, and stomach. The trocar's job in the embalming process is to suck out any fluids, gases, and waste in the body cavity. The brown liquid slid up the trocar's tube with an uncomfortable gurgling and sucking noise before splashing down the drain of the sink and into the sewers. Then the trocar reversed directions, no longer sucking but dumping more salmon-pink cocktail, of an even stronger chemical concentration this time, into the chest cavity and abdomen. If there had been any doubt Cliff was dead, the trocar dispelled it.

Bruce remained stoic as he violently jabbed Cliff with the trocar. Like Chris, who compared transporting bodies to 'moving furniture,' Bruce saw embalming as a trade that he had mastered over many years. It wouldn't do to be invested emotionally in every body. Bruce was able to perform this trocar work with no hesitation, all the while chatting with me like we were two old friends having a cup of coffee.

'Caitlin, you know what I need to figure out?' Stab. 'Those damn doves. You know what I'm talking about, those white doves that they release at the funerals?' Stab. 'That's where the money is, for sure. I gotta get some doves.' Stab, stab, stab.

There was, no doubt, a practical element to the embalming procedures of the Civil War. Families wanted to see the bodies of their dead relatives — an important aspect of ritual and closure. Embalming provided that opportunity. Even today the process can still be helpful for the corpse-about-town. As Bruce put it, 'Look, do you need embalming? No. But if you want him to have a big *Weekend at Bernie's*-style day, moving to different services and churches around the city, that body better be embalmed.' But the procedure didn't make sense for Cliff, who was going directly into the ground the next day at the veterans' cemetery in Sacramento.

When we speak of embalming, the stakes are not small. Though there is no law that requires it, embalming is the primary procedure in North America's billion-dollar funeral industry. It is the process around which the entire profession has revolved over the last 150 years. Without it, undertakers might still be the guys selling coffins, renting hearses, and pulling teeth on the side.

So how did we get to the place where we venerate embalming, decorating our dead as lurid, painted props on fluffy pillows, like poor Papa Aquino? The place where we embalm a man like Cliff as standard procedure, not bothering to question whether he needs it? Undertakers in the late nineteenth century realised that the corpse was their missing link to professionalism. The corpse could, and *would*, become a product.

Auguste Renouard, one of the earliest American embalmers, said in 1883 that 'the public had once believed that any fool could become an undertaker. Embalming, however, makes people marvel at the 'mysterious' and 'incomprehensible' process of preservation, and made them respect the practitioner.'

During embalming's early years, the public perceived the undertaker as a fool, since the profession required no national standards or qualifications. Roving 'professors' travelled from town to town holding three-day courses that ended with the professor attempting to sell you embalming fluid from the manufacturer he represented.

But in just a few decades the embalmer went from a huckster making money on the battlefield to a 'specialist.' Manufacturers of embalming chemicals aggressively marketed the image of the embalmer as a highly trained professional and a technical mastermind — an expert in both sanitation and the arts, creating beautiful corpses for public admiration. Nowhere else were art and science so expertly combined. Companies pleaded their case in trade magazines like *The Shroud, The Western Undertaker,* and *The Sunnyside.*

The new guard of embalming undertakers began to outline a new narrative: that with their technical training they protected the public from disease, and through their art they created a final 'memory picture' for the family. Sure, they made money off the dead. But so did doctors. Did not embalmers also deserve to be paid for their good work? Never mind that corpses had been kept quite safely in the home, prepared by the family, for hundreds of years. Embalming was what made the professionals professional — it was the magic ingredient.

Shinmon Aoki, a modern undertaker in Japan, described being ridiculed by society for his job washing and casketing the dead. His family disowned him and his wife wouldn't sleep with him because he was 'defiled' by corpses. So Aoki purchased a surgical robe, mask, and gloves and began showing up to homes dressed in full medical garb. People began responding differently; they bought the image he was selling and called him 'doctor.' The American undertaker had done something similar: by making themselves 'medical' they became legitimate.

Watching Cliff go through the embalming process, I thought back to the Huang family's witness cremation and the vow I'd made to be the one to cremate the members of my family.

'I've been thinking about this, Bruce,' I said, 'and I think I could cremate my mother, but there's no way in hell I could embalm her like this.'

To my surprise, he agreed. 'No way, *no way*. Maybe you think you could, till you see her layin' there *dead* on the table. You think you can slice your mom's neck and get to the vein? Think you could trocar her? This is your *mother* we're talking about. You'd have to be a tough sister to do that.'

Then Bruce stopped working, looked me in the eyes, and said something that made me think, and not for the last time, that he saw his work as more than a trade. Though he hid his ideas under a boisterous personality and get-rich-through-funeral-doves schemes, Bruce was a philosopher. 'Think of it this way: your mom's stomach is where you lived for nine months, it's how you got into this world, it's your origin, where you came from. Now you're gonna trocar that? Stab her? Destroy where you came from? You really wanna go there?'

High in the mountains of Tibet, where the ground is too rocky for burial and trees too scarce to provide wood for cremation pyres, Tibetans have developed another method of dealing with their dead. A professional *rogyapa*, or body breaker, slices the flesh off the corpse and grinds the remaining bones with barley flour and yak butter. The body is laid out on a high, flat rock to be eaten by vultures. The birds swoop in, carrying the body in all different directions, up into the sky. It is a generous way to be disposed of, the leftover flesh nourishing other animals.

Every culture has death rituals with the power to shock the uninitiated and challenge our personal web of significance — from the Wari' roasting the flesh of their fellow tribesmen to the Tibetan monk torn apart by the beaks of vultures to the long, silver trocar stabbing Cliff's intestines. But there is a crucial difference between what the Wari' did and the Tibetans do with their deceased compared to what Bruce did to Cliff. The difference is belief. The Wari' had belief in the importance of total bodily destruction. Tibetans have the belief that a body can sustain other beings after the soul has left it. Americans *practise* embalming, but we do not *believe* in embalming. It is not a ritual that brings us comfort; it is an additional $900 charge on our funeral bills. The US may be the biggest offender in this regard, but there is a growing desire in UK funeral homes to find a way to slip 'hygienic treatment' (an entertaining new addition to the roster of embalming euphemisms) onto their funeral bills as well.

If embalming were something a tradesman like Bruce would never perform on his own mother, I wondered why we were performing it on anyone at all.

Demon Babies

The nightmare revealer of madness unknown,
Of foetuses cooked for the Satanists' feast,
Old witches look on as a baby reveals,
A stretch of her leg to the lust of the Beast.

CHARLES BAUDELAIRE
Beacon Lights

When you graduate from college with a degree in medieval history, shockingly few employers come knocking at your door. Type 'medieval' and 'historian' into Craigslist, and the best career option you'll find is mead wench at Medieval Times. Really, your only choice is to go to graduate school and spend another seven years toiling away among dusty piles of illuminated manuscripts from thirteenth-century France. You squint at the faded Latin and develop a hunched back and pray that you can trick a university into letting you teach.

A career in academia had occurred to me, but I had neither the intellect nor the stamina for it. It was a cold, harsh world outside the confines of the ivory tower, and all I had to show for my years of college was a fifty-page bachelor's thesis titled: 'In Our Image: The Suppression of Demonic Births in Late Medieval Witchcraft Theory.'

My thesis — which at the time I considered to be my life's great masterwork — centred on the late medieval witch trials. When I speak of witches, I don't mean greeting-card Halloween witches with warts and black pointy hats. I mean women (and men) who were accused of sorcery in the late Middle Ages and then burned at the stake. Those witches. The numbers are fuzzy, but conservative historical estimates have well over 50,000 people executed in Western Europe for crimes of *maleficium*, the practice of harmful magic. And those 50,000 were just the people who were actually *executed* for witchcraft: burned, hanged, drowned, tortured, and so on. Countless more were accused of witchcraft and put on trial for their supposed crimes.

These people — the majority of whom were women — were not accused of simple, entry-level sorcery like lucky rabbits' feet or love potions. They were accused of nothing less than making a pact with Satan to spread death and destruction. Since Europe was largely illiterate, the only way an aspiring witch could seal a deal with the devil was through a sexual act — an erotic signature, of sorts.

Beyond wantonly giving themselves to Satan at a black Mass, accused witches were thought to raise storms, kill crops, make men impotent, and take the lives of infants. Any uncontrollable event in medieval- and Reformation-era Europe might very well have been a witch's doing.

It is easy for someone in the twenty-first century to be dismissive and declare, 'Dang, those medieval folk are so crazy with their flying demonic minions and sex pacts.' Yet witchcraft was as real to medieval men or women as the Earth being round or smoking causing cancer is real to us. It didn't matter whether they lived in a city or a small village, whether they were a lowly peasant farmer or the pope himself. They knew that there *were* witches and the witches *were* killing babies and crops and having lewd sex with the devil.

One of the best-known books of the 1500s was a witch-hunting manual by an inquisitor named Heinrich Kramer. The *Malleus Maleficarum*, or Hammer of the Witches, was the go-to guide for finding and getting rid of witches in your town. It is in this book that we learn, supposedly from a first-hand account of a witch in Switzerland, what witches did with the newborn infants:

113

This is the manner of it. We set our snares chiefly for unbaptised infants . . . and with our spells we kill them in their cradles or even when they are sleeping by their parents' side, in such a way that afterwards [they] are thought to have been overlain or to have died some other natural death. Then we secretly take them from their graves, and cook them in a cauldron, until the whole flesh comes away from the bones to make a soup which may easily be drunk. Of the more solid matter we make an unguent which is of virtue to help us in our arts and pleasures and in transportation.

According to the confessions of accused witches — most of which were obtained through extensive torture — the malefactors did all manner of things with their murdered infants. A little boiling, a little roasting, a little drinking of their blood. Most popular was grinding their leftover bones into salves to rub on their broomsticks in order to make them fly.

I bring up the history of witches killing babies to illustrate that I was writing about dead babies before I had ever really seen one. When you begin a new part of your life, you think you're leaving the older part behind.

'To hell with you, medieval witchy academic theory; to hell with your death philosophy, you wonky pedantic bastards! No more writing things that no one will ever read; I live in practice now! I sweat and ache and burn bodies and reveal tangible results!' Really though, there is never a way to leave the past behind. My poor dead witch babies came right along with me.

As I mentioned, the first thing you would notice when walking into the refrigeration unit at Westwind Cremation were the orderly stacks of brown cardboard boxes, each one labelled and filled with a recently (or not so recently) dead human. What you might *not* see at first are the adults' tragic little doppelgängers, the babies. They are spread out on a separate metal shelf in the back corner, a little garden of sadness. The older babies are wrapped in thick blue plastic. When you remove the plastic, they often looked just as babies should — little stocking caps and heart pendants and mittens. 'Just sleeping' . . . if they weren't so cold.

The younger babies — foetuses, if we're being more accurate — were no bigger than your hand. Too small for the blue plastic wrap, they float in plastic containers of brown formaldehyde like a middle-school science experiment. In English, with our plentiful euphemisms for difficult subjects, we say a child like this is stillborn, but speakers of other languages are rather more blunt: *nacido muerto, totge-boren, mort-né* — 'born dead.'

These babies arrived at the crematorium from the largest hospitals in Berkeley and Oakland. The hospitals would offer parents a free cremation if their baby died in utero or shortly after birth. It's a generous offer on the hospitals' part: cremations for babies, while often discounted by funeral homes, can still run to several hundred dollars. Regardless, it is the absolute last thing a mother wants the hospital to give her for free.

We would pick the babies up and bring them to our little garden: sometimes only three or four a week, sometimes quite a few more. We would cremate on a per-foetus basis and the hospitals would send us a cheque. Unlike the procedure for an adult, the hospitals would file the babies' death certificates with the state of California before the bodies even arrived at our crematorium. This kept us from having to ask a newly bereaved mother the required bureaucratic questions ('When was your last period? Did you smoke during your pregnancy? How many packs a day?').

Once, when Chris was across the Bay in San Francisco picking up a body at the

Coroner's Office, Mike told me I was being sent to fetch the week's babies. I asked Mike for very specific instructions. The job seemed horribly easy to mess up.

'You just pull the van up to the back loading dock and go into the nurses' station and tell them you're there for the babies. They should have the paperwork and stuff there; this one's easy,' Mike promised.

Ten minutes later I pulled the van into the loading dock behind the hospital and removed my gurney. It was a bit of a farce to use a full-sized adult gurney for a few babies, but I didn't think walking through the corridors with my arms filled with them was a particularly good plan either. I had an image of fumbling and dropping them, like a stressed-out mom carrying too many grocery bags to avoid the extra trip in from the car.

Per Mike's instructions, my first stop was the nurses' station. At this point, addressing the topic of death was still a struggle for me. My natural inclination when meeting new people is a warm smile and a little small talk, but when the goal is to collect baby corpses, any smile seems gauche and out of place. 'How are you today? I'm here for the baby corpses. By the way, girl, your earrings are *fabulous*.' On the other hand, if you keep your head bowed and your hands crossed and glumly state your reason for being there, you become the creepy girl from the funeral home. A delicate balance is required: happy but not *too* happy.

After the nurses conferred and decided I had the proper authority to abscond with the babies, I was escorted by security to the hospital morgue. The security guard was a stern woman who knew my dastardly purpose and would have none of it. After several botched attempts and small slams into the wall, I successfully wheeled my gurney into the elevator and we began our awkward descent to the morgue.

The guard's first question was reasonable: 'Why do you have that gurney?'

'Well,' I replied, 'you know, um, for the babies — to get them out?'

Her reply was quick: 'The other guy brings a little cardboard box. Where's the other guy?'

A cardboard box. Bloody genius. A discreet, portable, and *sensible* multi-baby conveyance. Why had Mike not mentioned this? I had failed already.

The security guard unlocked the morgue to let me in and stood there with her arms crossed, her distaste palpable. The rows of identical stainless-steel coolers gave me no inkling of where the babies might be hiding. As much as it pained me, I was forced to enquire where they were.

'You don't know?' came her response. She slowly raised a single finger, pointing to a cooler. She proceeded to watch as I removed the babies one by one and strapped them to the gurney in the most nonsensical way possible. I silently prayed my fairy death-mother would magically turn my gurney into a cardboard box or a milk crate or *something* so I wouldn't have to roll these formaldehyde foetuses down the hall on a gurney made for a full-sized adult.

I thought I was going to be able to slink away with my babies, head hung low but dignity intact. And then, she dealt the final blow: 'Ma'am, you're gonna need to sign for those.' Had I remembered to bring a pen? No, no I had not.

Noticing several pens hanging from the guard's shirt pocket, I asked, 'Well, could I borrow your pen?' Then came the look — perhaps the most derisive, scornful look that has ever been directed at me. As if I had personally taken the lives of each one of these infants with zero regret.

'Maybe when you take those gloves off,' she said, looking at my hand, still covered with baby-transferring rubber gloves.

To be fair, I'm not sure I would want to hand over my pen (precious commodity in a bureaucracy like an American hospital) to a girl who had just been handling baby corpses. But the way she said it gave me palpable knowledge of this woman's fear of death. It didn't matter how many times I smiled at her, expressed my new-on-the-job status with bumbling Hugh Grant-esque apologies. This woman had decided that I was dirty and deviant. Handmaiden to the underworld. Her regular duties as a security guard didn't faze her, but these trips to the morgue were too much. I removed the gloves, signed the release papers, and pushed the babies out to my van, a sad excuse for a final stroller ride.

Infant cremations were carried out in much the same way as adult cremations. We logged their names, if they even had names. Often they would be labelled only as 'Baby Johnson' or 'Baby Sanchez.' It was sadder when they had full names, even when they were something terrible, like Caitlin spelled Kate-Lynne. Full names showed how ready their parents were for them to be born and become a part of the family.

There is no mechanical loading device to deposit babies neatly into the chamber's fiery arms, as there is for adults. You, the crematorium operator, had to perfect the toss: the baby leaving your hand and coming to rest right below the main flame as it shot down from the ceiling of the retort. You had to make sure the baby landed in the sweet spot. With practice, you came to be very good at it.

Baby cremations were done at the end of the workday. The bricks lining the chamber grew so hot by the end of the day that the tiny babies practically cremated themselves. It was not uncommon for Mike to ask me to forgo cremating another adult and 'knock out a couple of babies' before the end of the day.

Adults could take hours to cremate, including the cremation itself and the cool-down process. Babies cremated in twenty minutes, tops. I found myself setting goals: *All right, Caitlin, it's what? Three fifteen p.m.? I bet you can do five babies before five o'clock. C'mon, girl, five before five. You get after that goal!*

Appalling? Absolutely. But if I let myself be sucked into the sorrow surrounding each foetus — each wanted but wasted tiny life — I'd go crazy. I'd end up like the security guard from the hospital: humourless and afraid.

I was a big proponent of unwrapping the larger babies, the ones kept in the blue plastic. I opened them not to gawk or engage in macabre curiosity. It just seemed wrong to not look at them — to toss them in like they never existed, like it was easier to pretend they were medical waste, hardly worth a second thought.

More than once I opened the plastic and received the garish surprise of a deformity: an enlarged head, overlapping eyes, a twisted mouth. In Europe before the Enlightenment, deformities aroused all manner of colourful explanations, including the mother's corrupt nature or the combination of the mother and father's evil thoughts. The child's monstrosity was a reflection of its parents' sin.

Ambroise Paré gave a long list of reasons for birth defects in his mid-sixteenth-century treatise *Des monstres et prodiges*: the wrath of God, an excess of semen, problems of the womb, and immodest cravings of the mother. These reasons seem irrelevant today, unless you count serious drug abuse while pregnant as an 'immodest craving' (which may indeed describe it perfectly).

Many such babies were clearly unwanted, their mere existence a burden. They were not all the precious apples of their parents' eyes who happened to go wrong somewhere in the biological trip from foetus to baby. Oakland has a much higher poverty rate than California as a whole — there are drugs, there are gangs. The babies came to Westwind in all colours and races; nefarious behaviour touches many communities in Oakland.

The deformed babies stared up with twisted features. I always wondered if they were the victims of the cruel caprices of biology or the products of mothers whose addictions and lifestyles were unstoppable even with a child growing inside them. It did no good to try to guess which was correct, though sometimes insight came months later when, after multiple phone calls, there was still no one willing to come pick up the baby's ashes.

I only wept once. It was for an older infant. I went into the office one afternoon to ask Mike what I could do while I waited for my current victims to cremate. His reply was, 'You know actually, you could maybe . . . yeah, you know what, never mind.'

'Wait, what do you mean, never mind?' I asked.

'I was gonna say you should go shave the hair off that baby, but don't worry, I'm not gonna make you do that.'

'No, I can do it!' I said, still frantic to prove my death-acceptance moxie.

The baby, a girl, was already eleven months old when she died of a heart defect. She was heavy, fully identifiable as a creature of the world. Her parents wanted her hair before she was cremated, hopefully to save and put in a locket or ring in the style of the Victorians. I admired the way people used to make beautiful jewellery and mementos out of the hair of the dead. We've lost that tradition somewhere along the way, and it is now considered gross to keep any part of the dead, even something as harmless as hair.

I had to cradle this infant's little body in my arms by logistical necessity, it being the best angle to clip and shave the tiny blonde curls from her head. I put the locks in an envelope and walked the baby into the crematorium. As I stood before the cremation machine, about to place her in, all of a sudden I started to cry — a rarity in this industrial work environment where efficiency is essential.

Why did this particular baby fill me with such woe?

Maybe it was because I had just shaved her head and wrapped her in a blanket and was about to consign her to the cremation flames, performing a hallowed ritual from some imaginary place. A place where a young woman is chosen to collect dead babies, shave their heads, and then burn them for the good of society.

Maybe it was because she was beautiful. With little bow lips and chubby cheeks, she looked like a 1950s Gerber baby in every way it is possible to look like the Gerber baby while also being dead.

Maybe she acted as a symbol for every other baby I didn't cry for. Those I didn't have time to cry for if I wanted to do my job and cremate five before five.

Or maybe it was because her blue eyes reminded me in some primal, narcissistic way of myself, and the fact that I somehow lived not to be cremated but to cremate. My heart beat and hers did not.

I could see why Mike wanted to delegate the baby-hair shaving to me, even if he hesitated to make the request. Mike had a son of his own, an angelic five-year-old boy. The process of cremating children was hard enough for a childless twenty-three-year-old, but it had to be torture for a loving father. He never said it, but there were times when his veneer would crack ever so slightly, when you could see that it affected him.

Months had passed with me believing Mike was pure hard-ass. But the ogre Mike I had created in my head wasn't anything close to the actual Mike. Actual Mike had a New-Agey wife named Gwaedlys, an adorable young child, and an organic garden in his backyard. He had taken the job at the crematorium after years of working to secure amnesty for refugees. I viewed him as an ogre because no matter how hard I worked he remained stern, unimpressed by my efforts. It wasn't that Mike gave me negative feedback, but the absence of feedback was just as crippling for an insecure Millennial. I projected onto him the fear that a weakling like me couldn't handle the work, couldn't handle the real death I had been so desperate to be in the presence of.

I asked Bruce about Mike not wanting to handle the babies. He looked at me like I was crazy for even asking. 'Well, yeah, duh Mike wants you to do it; he's got a kid. You don't have a kid. You see your baby in that baby. When you get older your own mortality starts to creep in on you. Watch out, children are going to bother you the older you get,' he said, as if in warning.

When my Gerber baby was done cremating, all that was left of her — all that was left of any of the babies we cremated — was a tiny pile of ash and bone fragments. The bones of a baby are too small to be reduced to powder in the same Cremulator (bone grinder) used for adults. But cultural expectations (and again, the law) dictated that we couldn't return a tiny sack of identifiable, obvious bones to the parents either. So after the bones cooled down, each baby had to be 'processed' by hand. Using a small piece of metal like a wee pestle, I ground their little femurs and skull fragments until they were uniform. The bones produced maybe an eighth of a cup of cremated remains, but the parents could bury them, put them in a mini urn, scatter them, hold them in their hands.

I had written my thesis on medieval witches accused of roasting dead infants and grinding their bones. A year later I found myself literally roasting dead infants and grinding their bones. The tragedy of the women who were accused of witchcraft was that they never actually ground the bones of babies to help them fly to a midnight devil's Sabbath. But they were unjustly killed for it anyway, burned alive at the stake. I, on the other hand, did grind the bones of babies. Often I was thanked by their poor parents for my care and concern.

Things change.

Direct Disposal

Mark Nguyen was only thirty years old when he died. His body was under cold storage awaiting an autopsy at the San Francisco Medical Examiner's Office when his mother arrived to arrange his cremation at Westwind.

'For the death certificate — was Mark married, Mrs. Nguyen?'

'No, dear, he wasn't.'

'Did he have children?'

'No, he didn't.'

'And what was Mark's most recent career?'

'No, he didn't have one of those. He never worked.'

'I'm so sorry Mrs. Nguyen,' I said, thinking a woman with a dead thirty-year-old son would be understandably destroyed.

'Oh, honey,' she said, shaking her head in resignation, 'trust me, it's for the best.'

Mrs. Nguyen had done her mourning for her son long ago: when he first started using drugs, first went to jail, had his first . . . second . . . sixth relapse. Every time Mark went missing she worried he had overdosed. Just two days earlier she had found Mark dead on the floor in a rent-by-the-hour motel room in the Tenderloin District of San Francisco. After discovering his body, she no longer had to worry. Her worst fears had come true — and she was relieved.

When it came time to pay for the cremation, Mrs. Nguyen handed me a credit card, pulled it back, and said, 'Wait, hold on hon, use this one instead. I get airline miles on it. At least Mark can get me some miles.'

'You should go somewhere tropical,' I blurted without thinking, as if she had come to see a travel agent. After all, when you find your son deceased in a seedy motel room, don't you deserve a mai tai?

'I think that would be lovely, dear,' she said, signing her receipt. 'I've always wanted to go to Kauai.'

'I'm from Oahu originally, but I've really come to like the Hilo side of the Big Island,' I replied, and we slipped into a natural conversation about the pros and cons of the different Hawaiian islands that Mrs. Nguyen could visit on her son Mark's cremation miles.

Mrs. Nguyen's was my first airline miles request, but Westwind Cremation & Burial was no stranger to the marriage of technology and death. Inside Westwind's garage, on the wall above the extra boxes of urns, hung the framed city business licence for Bayside Cremation. The garage *technically* stood at a different street address, and Bayside Cremation was *technically* a different business, but they operated out of the same facility. Bayside distinguished itself by offering the cutting-edge option of ordering a cremation over the Internet.

If your father died in a local hospital, you could visit the Bayside Cremation website, type in the location of Dad's body, print out some forms, sign them, fax them back to the number provided, and input your credit card number to the website. All of this without ever having to speak to a real person. In fact, you weren't allowed to speak to a real person even if you wanted to: all questions had to be sent by e-mail to info@baysidecremation.com. Two weeks later, the doorbell would ring and the postman would hand over Dad's ashes, shipped by registered mail, signature required. No funeral home, no sad faces, no need to see Dad's body — total avoidance for the low, low price of $799.99.

Nothing was different behind the scenes, mind you. Either Chris or I still went to pick up the body, still filed the death certificate, still cremated in the same cremation machine. Bayside Cremation offered Westwind's model of direct cremation — already pretty low on human interaction — minus the human interaction altogether.

Bruce, our embalmer, had strong feelings

about the need for actual live humans to take care of dead humans: 'Look, Caitlin, a computer can't cremate a body.' He had worked at another cremation facility before Westwind, where they had the workers run the cremation machines off computerised timers. 'You'd think that's a good idea, right, for efficiency and whatnot? But it wouldn't work if that body wasn't in there perfect. If it wasn't perfect, that machine goes, 'Oh, ding-ding, cremation is over!' and that body ain't cremated. Open it up, there's a half-charred body in there. That's what you get with a computer, man.'

Most of the families who chose to use Bayside Cremation were looking for the rock-bottom price at which to dispose of their sixty-five-year-old estranged brother-in-law whose arrangements California legally required them to pay for. Mark Nguyen might have been an ideal Bayside Cremation case, a long-term drug addict with a mother who had mentally buried him long before his actual death. But there were troubling cases, too. One gentleman cremated by Bayside was just twenty-one — close to my age at the time. Twenty-one years is time enough to be a fuck-up, sure, but not time enough to be a lost cause.

I tried to imagine my parents receiving word of my death. My mother would turn to my father and say, 'Now, John, I wonder if we could find an inexpensive online cremation for Caiti? Remember how easy it was to order the Chinese food online last week? Since I don't need to discuss any questions or concerns about my precious offspring with an actual human being, I'm sure the Internet option will be just fine.'

I was beginning to doubt that my own body would be well cared for were I to die young. The very idea of Bayside Cremation crushed me with loneliness. I was burdened with the thought that any of my Facebook friends would be quick to comment 'Yummy!' on a photo of my Niçoise salad, but wouldn't step up to wipe the sweat from my dying brow or the poop off my corpse.

It was my job to wrap up the Bayside Cremation ashes for mailing. The United States Postal Service required that the urns be packaged a certain way, with heavy brown packing tape covering all sides and what felt like forty separate labels. When there were several packages ready to be mailed I'd trundle into the post office and set them out on the counter. The elderly Asian lady behind the counter shook her head at me while covering the boxes with the 'Human Remains' stamp.

'Look, the families want them sent, I don't make the rules!' I insisted.

Her judgemental expression didn't soften, she just continued to stamp. Stamp. Stamp.

Even with the mailing boxes sealed, boxed, and taped up like a citadel, we still had family members trying to convince us they received them in poor condition. *Anything* to avoid paying. One gentleman in Pennsylvania claimed his brother had arrived in a package actively leaking remains, a situation that deteriorated when he set his brother in the backseat of his convertible and ash flew out into the air as he drove down the interstate. While I appreciated the homage to *The Big Lebowski*, he gave up on his story and stopped threatening lawsuits when I told him how the urn was packaged. We came to find out he had never even gone to the post office to pick it up.

There was a special fax sound when a Bayside Cremation request came down through the Internet tubes. It elicited a Pavlovian response from Westwind employees because we had been promised a company cocktail party and dinner when we hit our first hundred online cremation cases.

One Tuesday morning the fax rang, and Chris stood up with his usual grumble (cocktail parties and social gatherings in general holding no appeal for him) and went over to pick it up.

'Oh, what the hell, Cat, she's nine.'

'Wait, Chris, she's what?'

'She's nine.'

'Like nine years old?' I asked, horrified. 'What's her name? Jessica?'

'Ashley,' Chris said, shaking his head. 'Jesus.'

A nine-year-old girl named Ashley, who had just finished the third grade, died at a hospital, where her parents left her body, went home, typed their credit card into a website, and waited two weeks for her to appear in a box by mail.

I did end up talking to Ashley's mother on the phone, because no matter how many e-mails we sent back and forth, the credit card she provided wouldn't work. It turned out she had been trying to use her Sears department store card to pay for the cremation. Who, really, is to say that Sears won't offer a similar one-click cremation in the future? If they do, they will surely think of a euphemism for cremation like 'heat fragmentation procedure' to spare us the reality of the offer. Perhaps Ashley's family members were death visionaries of the future, not the thoughtless people I made them out to be.

The idea that a nine-year-old girl can magically transform into a neat, tidy box of remains is ignorant and shameful for our culture. It is the equivalent of grown adults thinking that babies come from storks. But Joe, Westwind's owner, thought Bayside Cremation was the future of low-cost death care. It wouldn't be the first time California had witnessed the future of death.

⋆ ⋆ ⋆

Just north of Los Angeles is the city of Glendale, home to such diverse offerings as one of the largest populations of Armenians in the United States, the Baskin-Robbins ice-cream chain, and arguably one of the most important cemeteries in the world — Forest Lawn. Forest Lawn is not just a cemetery, but a 'memorial park,' with expansive, rolling hills and nary a headstone in sight. Its soil houses a Who's Who of Hollywood celebrities: Clark Gable, Jimmy Stewart, Humphrey Bogart, Nat King Cole, Jean Harlow, Elizabeth Taylor, Michael Jackson, and even Walt Disney himself (despite the legend, he was not cryogenically frozen).

Founded in 1906, Forest Lawn got a new general manager in 1917 named Hubert Eaton, a businessman with a forceful dislike of the drab European model of death. His vision was to create a new, optimistic, American 'memorial park,' waging an all-out war against traditional cemeteries, which he called 'depressing stoneyards.' Eaton removed Forest Lawn's headstones and replaced them with flat identification markers, as 'you wouldn't want to mar [the cemetery] with tombstones. It would spoil everything.' He littered the grounds of Forest Lawn with art and sculptures, which he referred to as his 'silent salesmen.' His first major purchase was a sculpture called *Duck Baby*, a naked toddler surrounded by ducklings. As Forest Lawn's artistic acquisitions grew, he offered one million lire to the Italian artist who could paint him 'a Christ filled with radiance and looking upward with an inner light of joy and hope.' To be more specific, Eaton wanted 'an American-faced Christ.'

Eaton was the original upbeat undertaker. His goal was 'to erase all signs of mourning.' Forest Lawn was the genesis of some of the American funeral industry's most beloved death-denial euphemisms. Death became 'leave-taking,' a corpse became 'the loved one,' 'the remains,' or 'Mr. So-and-So,' who, after elaborate embalming and cosmetic treatment, awaited burial in a private, well-furnished 'slumber' room.

An article in a 1959 issue of *Time* called

Forest Lawn the 'Disneyland of Death,' and described Eaton as starting his day off by leading his staff in prayer and reminding them that 'they were selling immortality.' There were, of course, limits to who would be allowed to purchase immortality. The same article tells us that 'Negroes and Chinese were regretfully refused.'

Forest Lawn became well known for its aggressive, beautiful-death-at-all-costs policy, satirised in Evelyn Waugh's *The Loved One*. Waugh described in verse how Eaton's army of luxury embalmers ensured that every corpse coming to Forest Lawn was 'pickled in formaldehyde and painted like a whore, / Shrimp-pink incorruptible, not lost or gone before.'

Hubert Eaton implemented his plan for the beautiful death with a dictatorial air. He was known to his employees (by his own decree) as 'The Builder.' (This reminds me of the surreal nomenclature of my middle-school orthodontist, who had his dental assistants refer to him not as 'the doctor' or 'Dr. Wong' but just 'Doctor.' The title is still imprinted on my mind, though my teeth have long since migrated back to their original crooked configuration. 'Doctor will be with you in a minute,' or 'When is the last time you saw Doctor?' or 'I'll have to ask Doctor what he thinks about that . . . ')

Due in no small part to the influence of Forest Lawn, the 1950s was a glamorous time for the death industry. In the ninety years since the end of the Civil War, undertakers had managed to shift the public's perception of their occupation. They went from local coffinmakers forced to supplement their income in other ways to highly trained medical professionals, embalming bodies for the 'good of public health,' and creating artistic corpse displays for the family. It didn't hurt that the postwar economic boom gave people the expendable income to keep up with the postmortem Joneses.

For almost twenty years after the end of World War II, the national cremation rate hung out in the scandalously low 3 to 4 per cent range. Why would a family want a cremation when they could impress their neighbours with sleek Cadillac-style caskets, flower arrangements, embalming, and elaborate funerals? The embalmed body was art, heading down into the grave on pastel pillows in gauzy burial gowns with bouffant hairdos. It was pure kitsch, a perfect fit for the postwar aesthetic. Stephen Prothero, professor of religion and scholar of the American cremation industry explained, 'The 1950s represented a wonderful opportunity for gaudy excess.'

But the 'gaudy excess' could not last forever, and by the early 1960s, American consumers began to feel swindled by the funeral industry's absurdly high prices. Where once the funeral home was a pillar of righteousness in the community, people started to suspect that perhaps undertakers were unscrupulous charlatans taking advantage of grieving families. The undisputed leader of the movement against the funeral status quo was a woman named Jessica Mitford.

Mitford was a writer and journalist born into a wildly eccentric family of English aristocrats. She had four famous sisters, one of whom was a Nazi and a 'tremendous friend of Hitler.' Mitford influenced everyone from Christopher Hitchens to Maya Angelou. JK Rowling cited Mitford as her biggest influence as a writer.

In 1963, Mitford wrote a book called *The American Way of Death*, which was not at all kind to funeral directors. A card-carrying Communist, Mitford believed funeral directors were avaricious capitalists who had managed to 'perpetrate a huge, macabre, and expensive practical joke on the American public.' *The American Way of Death* was a massive bestseller, staying at the top of the *New York Times* bestseller list for weeks. In response to her book, Mitford received thousands of letters from citizens who felt cheated by the death industry. She found unlikely allies in Christian clergy members, who thought the focus on the expensive funeral was 'pagan.'

Mitford grudgingly admitted that Forest Lawn's Hubert Eaton 'probably had more influence on the trends of the modern cemetery industry than any other human being,' and thus, he was the funeral man she hated most.

To protest the evil wrought by Forest Lawn and their ilk, Mitford announced that when she died she would forgo the expensive 'traditional' funeral service and choose an inexpensive cremation instead. It is safe to say that 1963 was cremation's year. *The American Way of Death* came out in 1963, as did Pope Paul VI's overturning of the Catholic Church's ban on cremation. These two factors turned the death trends of the entire country towards cremation. When *The American Way of Death* came out, the vast majority of Americans were opting for embalming followed by burial. Rates of cremation have risen steadily in the years following Mitford's book, however. Sociologists believe 50 per cent of Americans, if not the majority, will choose it within the coming decade.

When Mitford died in 1996, her husband

made good on her request and sent her body for a direct cremation — $475.00 for a no-frills, straight cremation, with no funeral and no family present. Her ashes were placed in a disposable plastic urn. As Mitford saw it, a direct cremation was the clever, inexpensive way to go. The old-timers in the death industry — mostly men — called this type of direct cremation 'bake 'n' shake' or 'direct disposal.' Mitford's last request was one final dig at this group who hated everything she stood for.

Although she had grown up in England, Mitford's second husband was an American and they had been living for years in Oakland, California. So where did she get this $475.00 direct cremation? Good ol' Westwind Cremation & Burial. Chris picked up her body himself.

Working as the operator of the very cremation machine that had reduced Jessica Mitford to ash made me self-satisfied with my little place in death history. I knew that, like Mitford, I didn't agree with the large, expensive traditional funerals of the past. I wasn't sold on eternal preservation, either, despite Bruce's open enthusiasm for the art of embalming. It was an admirable thing for Mitford to pull back the 'formaldehyde curtain' of embalming and to reveal to the public that behind the scenes the average dead person was 'in short order sprayed, sliced, pierced, pickled, trussed, trimmed, creamed, waxed, painted, rouged, and neatly dressed — transformed from a common corpse into a Beautiful Memory Picture.'

She wasn't afraid to use vivid details, to the point where her original publisher warned her that she made the book 'harder to sell by going at too much length and in too gooey detail into the process of embalming.' To her credit, Mitford switched publishers and forged ahead.

But the longer I worked at Westwind, I found that I wasn't entirely in agreement with Mitford, though it felt like a betrayal to question her. After all, she was the undisputed queen of the alternative funeral industry, a crusader with a love for the consumer. If embalming and expensive funerals were bad, then surely her call for simple, affordable funerals must be good?

Yet I found something disturbing about a death culture based on direct cremation alone. Although Westwind offered embalmings and burials, the driving source of business was direct cremation — corpse to ashes for less than a thousand dollars. Now Bayside Cremation and Internet servicing had emerged as Mitford's greatest ally in the quest to cut out the funeral director.

On the cover of my copy of the 1998 reissue of *The American Way of Death*, Mitford sits in the hallway of an above-ground mausoleum. She wears a sensible suit, carries a sensible bag, and bears a sensible, no-nonsense expression. She is the middle-aged version of the stern woman featured on the television show *Supernanny*, where 'Nanny' has been imported from England to straighten out a brood of unruly American children who scream things like 'But Nanny, bacon is a vegetable!'

Mitford's Englishness was front and centre in her writing. She was proud of the traditions of her birthplace, traditions that in modern times meant precious little interaction with the body at the time of death. She quotes a fellow Englishwoman living in San Francisco who had attended an American wake where the body was viewed: 'It shook me rigid to get there and find the casket open and poor old Oscar lying there in his brown tweed suit, wearing a suntan make-up and just the wrong shade of lipstick. If I had not been extremely fond of the old boy, I have a horrible feeling that I might have giggled. Then and there I decided that I could never face another American funeral — even dead.'

Viewing the embalmed body evolved as the

cultural norm in the United States and Canada, but the Brits (at least among Mitford's fellow upperclassmen) chose a complete absence of the corpse. Perhaps that is an oversimplification. Just as the raucous jazz funerals of New Orleans challenge the idea of a unified American death, the wakes of Ireland challenge the idea of a unified British death. But the exception only proves the rule.

Geoffrey Gorer, the British anthropologist, compared modern death in Britain to a kind of pornography. Where sex and sexuality were the cultural taboo of the Victorian period, death and dying were the taboo of the modern world. 'Our great-grandparents were told that babies were found under gooseberry bushes or cabbages; our children are likely to be told that those who have passed on . . . are changed into flowers, or lie at rest in lovely gardens.'

Gorer argued that the 'natural deaths' of disease and old age were replaced in the twentieth century by 'violent deaths' — wars, concentration camps, car accidents, nuclear weapons. If the American optimism led to a prettying-up of the corpse with make-up and chemicals, British pessimism led to the removal of the corpse and the death ritual from polite society.

In Mitford's foreword to *The American Way of Death*, two things struck me. First was her statement that the book wouldn't go into the 'quaint death customs still practised by certain Indian tribes.' Customs that, incidentally, were far from quaint. Native Americans had intensely rich death rituals including the Dakota Sioux's method of building six-to-eight-foot-tall wooden platforms and depositing the body for exposure to the elements in an elaborate mourning ceremony. Second was Mitford's firm dismissal that the American public might be partially to blame for the way things had become in the funeral industry. She states confidently: 'I am unwilling on the basis of present evidence to find the public guilty.'

Unlike Mitford, I *was* willing to find the public guilty. Very willing, in fact.

Arranging a funeral at Westwind, the daughter of a deceased woman looked me deeply in the eyes and said, 'This planning is so difficult, only because Mother's death was so unexpected. You have to understand, she had only been on hospice for six months.'

This woman's mother had been on hospice (end-of-life care) for *six months*. That's 180 days of your mother actively dying in your home. You knew she was ill *long* before she went into hospice care. Why did you not look

145

up the best funeral homes in the area, compare prices, ask friends and family, figure out what's legal, or most important, *talk to your mother about what she herself wanted when she died?* Your mother was dying and you damn well knew it. Refusing to talk about it and then calling it 'unexpected' is not an acceptable excuse.

When a young person dies unexpectedly, the family will likely face what Mitford called the 'necessity of buying a product of which they are totally ignorant.' The sudden death of a young person is a horrible tragedy. In their sorrow, the family should not have to worry that a funeral home will take advantage and upsell them to a more expensive casket or funeral-service package. But anyone who works in the death industry can readily tell you that a slim minority of cases involves the sudden death of a young person. Most deaths come after long, significant diseases or very lengthy lives.

If I showed up at a used-car lot and the salesman said, 'It's $45,000 for this 1996 Hyundai' (market value $4,200) and I bought it, the situation would be my fault. I could shake my fist all I wanted at the con artist who sold me the $45,000 Hyundai, but everyone would agree that I had been taken advantage of because I did not do my research.

Mitford acknowledged that the average person in the market for a car would read *Consumer Reports* (or, in the twenty-first century, presumably browse the Internet). But to do that kind of research into the death industry, well, 'it just would not seem right.' Because the average person does not like to think about the implications of death, 'he is anxious to get the whole thing over with.' At no point does Mitford object to this head-in-the-sand approach.

The American Way of Death assures readers that hating death is perfectly normal: Of *course* you're anxious to get the whole thing over with and leave the funeral home; of *course* it would be morbid to go around asking in advance what 'reliable undertakers' people use; of *course* you don't know what a funeral home looks like or how it runs. Mitford promised us in her soothing prose that our death denial was not only appropriate, it was the natural state of affairs. She was an enabler.

Mitford hated the fact that funeral directors were businesspeople. But for better or worse, that's what they are. Funeral homes in most developed countries are money-making private enterprises. People working in corporate funeral homes have no shortage of stories to tell of the overwhelming pressure to sell and push extra products and services. A former funeral director from one of the major corporate funeral homes told me that when he had a bad month in revenues (perhaps because his clientele that month came from lower-income families or because his clients had chosen cremation), 'all of a sudden there was corporate in Texas on the phone asking if something was wrong in your life, asking if you understood you wouldn't be getting your bonus.'

As a journalist, Mitford was an expert at stirring things up, exposing the hidden wrongs of the world. There is no doubt that the American funeral industry needed a change. What it got, however, was a scorched-earth policy. Mitford lit a match, threw it over her shoulder, and walked away. In her wake, she left a disgruntled public clamouring for cheaper funeral alternatives.

In writing *The American Way of Death*, Jessica Mitford wasn't trying to improve our relationship with death, she was trying to improve our relationship with the price point. That is where she went wrong. It was *death* that the public was being cheated out of by the funeral industry, not money. The realistic interaction with death and the chance to face our own mortality. For all of Mitford's good intentions, direct cremation has only made the situation worse.

Unnatural Natural

'How dare you try to charge us that?' she screamed in a thick Eastern European accent.

'I'm sorry, Ms. Ionescu,' I tried to explain, 'but we have to charge you the hundred and seventy-five dollars.'

Ms. Ionescu, daughter of the late Elena Ionescu, sat in front of me at the Westwind Cremation arrangement desk. Her thick brown hair spiralled in corkscrew rings from the side of her head and her hands, loaded down with golden rings, gesticulated wildly.

'You are trying to extort us. I don't understand why you are doing this, I am just here to see my mother one last time.'

If this had been my first ride at the 'one last time' rodeo, I might have caved in to this woman's demands. As it was, I knew Mike wouldn't like me dropping the charge just because I hoped to avoid a confrontation. It was common for families to want to 'see Mom one last time' before she was cremated or buried. They didn't want to have to pay $175 for the privilege. It was hard to explain why we suggested they did.

Dead people look very, very dead. It is

difficult to grasp what that means, since it's unlikely that any of us will stumble across a roving pack of dead bodies in the wild. We live in a world where people rarely die in their homes, and if they do, they're carted off to the funeral home the second after taking their last breath. If a North American *has* seen a dead body, that body has likely been embalmed, made up, and dressed in its Sunday finest by a funeral-home employee.

Televised crime shows rarely help matters. The dead bodies on prime-time TV, discovered by maids, maintenance men, and joggers in Central Park, are laid out as if they have already been prepared for a wake, eyes closed and lips pursed together, glossed over with a whitish-blue-tinted make-up, which we, the viewers, read as 'dead.' The victims on these shows are played by young models and actors who are making their rounds on the *CSI* and *Law & Order* corpse circuit while waiting to get called for a pilot. They are a far cry from the majority of bodies in a funeral home — old, knotted, and wracked with years of diseases like cancer and cirrhosis of the liver.

There was a huge gap between what the Ionescu family *expected* and what the Ionescu family would actually *get* if we rolled Elena directly out of the refrigeration unit to visit with her waiting family. That gap of expectation has become a problem for funeral homes, under constant threat of being sued by families when a body doesn't look how they expect it to look. It is challenging, of course, to feel sorry for the funeral industry, as the rise of embalming was what created this gap in the first place.

Untreated, a dead person's face looks horrific, at least by our very narrow cultural expectations. Their droopy, open eyes cloud over in a vacant stare. Their mouths stretch wide like Edvard Munch's *The Scream*. The colour drains from their faces. These images reflect the normal biological processes of death, but they are not what a family wants to see. As part of their price lists, funeral homes generally charge anywhere from $175 to $500 for 'setting the features.' That is how corpses come to look 'peaceful,' 'natural,' and 'at rest.'

The cruel fact was that Elena Ionescu, a ninety-year-old Romanian woman, had been in the hospital for over two months prior to her death. The combination of being bedridden for eight weeks and hooked up to IV drips and machines had caused Elena's body to slide into full-blown oedema, a post-mortem condition in which fluid swells beneath the skin. She was puffed up like the Michelin man, oedema having taken over the lower parts of her legs, arms, and back. Her skin leaked fluid. What's worse, the overwhelming moisture from the oedema had expedited decomposition.

Where decomposition has begun and excess fluid abounds, the dreaded 'skin slip' becomes a real possibility. Its technical name is desquamation, but in practice it is called skin slip, a phrase that can be given credit for calling it like ya see it. The decomposition process had caused gas and pressure to build up inside Elena, her skin to loosen, and the top layer of skin to slip away, like it wanted to abandon ship. If this situation happened to a living person, the skin would eventually regrow and regenerate. For Elena, this was it: until cremation her skin would remain fresh, pink, and covered in a thin layer of slime.

It was safe to say that Elena's body would not look like her irate daughter imagined it would. Yet Westwind Cremation & Burial had absolutely no right to keep Elena Ionescu locked in our refrigeration unit. Corpses, by law, are quasi-property. Elena's family *owned* her dead body until burial or cremation. Which leads us to another popular reason to sue funeral homes — lawsuits arise after some scorned funeral director illegally holds a dead body as corpse collateral until the family can pay.

If Elena's daughter said, 'Hand her over

this instant, I'm putting Mother in the backseat of my car and driving away from this godless place,' I would have done it, no questions asked. There were days when I might have applauded such a decision.

'Ms. Ionescu, I'm sorry. You're absolutely welcome to go elsewhere, I encourage you to call around. But I think that you will find the hundred-and-seventy-five-dollar charge to be the case wherever you go in the area,' I said, making one last pitch.

'I guess we don't have a choice, do we?' she replied, her rings clanking together as she signed her name at the bottom of the contract.

Two hours later, Elena Ionescu was laid out before me on the preparation-room table, about to be made 'natural' for her viewing the next day. It is a not-so-well-kept funeral industry secret that the processes used to make someone appear natural are often highly *unnatural*.

I stood in front of the same metal cabinet where several months earlier Mike had presented me with my first corpse-shaving razor. I pulled out two 'eye caps,' which looked like small plastic spaceships, rounded and flesh-coloured. The tiny spikes sticking up from the plastic made it look like a miniature Inquisition-era torture device. The purpose of the eye caps was twofold: first, by placing a cap under Elena's eyelid, her eyes would appear rounded, masking the sunken, flattened eyeballs hiding below; second, the torture spikes served the important function of catching the back of the eyelids, preventing them from floating up into a postmortem wink.

With Q-tips and cotton I cleaned out Elena's nose, ears, and mouth — a deeply unpleasant task. In the last throes of life, basic hygiene is often ignored. This is reasonable, but reason does not make the aftermath any less abhorrent. In moving the corpse, there is always a chance there may be a sudden burst of 'purge' — a frothy, reddish-brown liquid expunged from the lungs and stomach. I did not envy nurses, whose living patients produced these disagreeable fluids every day.

Without her dentures, which had been left soaking in a glass by her hospital bed, Elena's lips had rolled in on empty gums. To counteract this, we used a mouth former, a curved piece of plastic that looked like a larger (mouth-shaped) eye cap. I gently lifted her upper lip to insert the mouth former, but the device was far too big for an elderly woman. It made her look like an ape, or a footballer wearing a mouth guard. Appalled, I quickly removed it and trimmed it down with a heavy pair of scissors.

Next came the needle injector. The needle injector was a mouth-closing gun, a metal device used to shoot wires into the decedent's gums so they could be tied together to hold the mouth shut. I began by choosing a sharp pin with a long wire attached to the end, like a tiny metal tadpole. It was placed into the tip of a large metal needle, which shot the barb into the top and bottom gums. Our injector at Westwind was of somewhat shoddy quality, a bit rusty. It didn't inject with the level of oomph one would desire. This meant I had to climb on top of Elena and use my whole body weight to inject the wires with a mighty 'Hoo-AH!'

At ninety years old, Elena was lacking in the gums department, necessitating several tries to get the barbs to stay put. Once the barbs were lodged in place, the two wire tadpole tails were twisted together through the plastic of the mouth former, bringing the upper and lower jaw together.

If all these tricks failed and the eyes or mouth still insisted on falling open, there was always the secret weapon: superglue. We used those little green tubes of liquid magic for everything. Even if, by some miracle, the eye caps and needle injector worked as intended, it was wise to reinforce. Milky blue eyes and exposed gums were not what the family wanted, but they were less terrifying than catching an unwanted glimpse of the flesh-toned spiked plastic or the thick tadpole wires that now held their loved one's face intact.

Once the Ionescu family had resigned themselves to paying the 'one last time' charge, they came back to Westwind with a set of clothes so we could dress Elena for her visitation. Not only had Elena's oedema swollen her to twice her normal size, her family — like many families — had brought in clothes from her fashionable, svelte past. There is a reason why the newspaper obituary pages are littered with glamour shots, wedding pictures, and portraits from long-ago debutante balls. We want people to remain forever in their prime like a beautiful rosy-cheeked Kate Winslet meeting Leonardo DiCaprio in *Titanic* heaven decades after the ship had sunk.

Mike had to help me squeeze Elena into her opulent, Glasnost-era Eastern European dress. He had a bag of helpful tricks, e.g., saran-wrapping her arms like a 1950s B-picture mummy. But the odyssey was not yet complete. As a general rule, if anyone ever asks you to put stockings on a ninety-year-old deceased Romanian woman with oedema, your answer should be no.

'Mike,' I said with a sigh, 'we know her lower half is going to be covered with the sheets during the visitation. I hate to say it, but we could probably forgo the stockings.'

Mike, to his credit as a professional, wasn't having it. 'Nope, the family paid for the dressing and viewing, man. We can get these on.'

As a business, the funeral industry has developed by selling a certain type of 'dignity.' Dignity is having a well-orchestrated final moment for the family, complete with a well-orchestrated corpse. Funeral directors become like directors for the stage, curating the evening's performance. The corpse is the star of the show and pains are taken to make sure the fourth wall is never broken, that the corpse does not interact with the audience and spoil the illusion.

Service Corporation International, the largest American funeral home and cemetery corporation, based in Houston, Texas, has even managed to trademark dignity. Go to any of their 'Dignity Memorial®' facilities, and that pesky ® shows up every time, subtly letting you know they've cornered the market on post-mortem poise.

At Elena's visitation the next morning, her

daughter pulled her hair and howled in grief. It was a genuine, haunting sound that I wanted to take in and appreciate as profound. But all I could focus on was the gnawing fear that an eye would slide open or a saran-wrapped arm would spring a leak. Elena looked pretty put-together, considering. Nevertheless, the farce of the experience had got to me. They say you can put lipstick on a pig and it's still a pig. The same holds true for a dead body. Put lipstick on a corpse and you've played dress-up with a corpse.

The Monday after Elena Ionescu's viewing, I came to work to find that, over the weekend, both cremation machines had received glorious new floors, smooth as a baby's bottom. Joe, the crematorium owner, put in a brief appearance to crawl inside the retort chamber with concrete, rebar, and proverbial balls of steel to complete the job himself. Mind you, I still had never met him, and this little weekend project fuelled his legendary status in my mind, as I couldn't fathom a living person wriggling himself (voluntarily!) into the cremation chamber. Prior to resurfacing, the floors had begun to resemble the topography of the Alps. Large chunks of concrete dislodged themselves from years of wear and tear. With the floors in this condition, sweeping out the bones and ashes had become a test of dexterity and will that outstripped the job description. With these new floors I could rake the bones out with graceful, luxurious strokes, and without even breaking a sweat.

Day one of freshly floored machines went off without a hitch. Day two began with me loading in Mrs. Greyhound. In marked contrast to her sleek surname, Mrs. Greyhound was a pleasantly plump woman in her eighties. Her permed white hair and soft hands reminded me of my paternal grandmother, a schoolteacher in a one-room schoolhouse in small-town Iowa who raised seven children and made cinnamon rolls from scratch. One summer when I was a child, I visited her in Iowa and was awoken in the middle of the night to find her crying in the dark living room because she knew 'that there are some people who don't know the love of Jesus.' My grandmother had died almost ten years before I began working at Westwind, but only my father had been able to fly back to Iowa for the funeral. It was easy to see your own grandmother in people ... well, bodies ... like Mrs. Greyhound.

Using the principles of Cremation 101, Mrs. Greyhound went in at the beginning of the day, when the cremation retorts were still cool. We needed the cremation chambers stone cold in the morning to accommodate our larger men and women. Without a cold chamber, the flesh would burn up too quickly, going up the smokestack in thick, dark puffs, potentially summoning the fire department. People with additional body fat (such as the zaftig Mrs. Greyhound) were cremated first, while smaller, older ladies with zero body fat (and babies) were generally saved for the end of the day.

I loaded Mrs. Greyhound into the cold retort and went about my morning business. When I returned moments later, there was smoke pouring out the door. Billowing, black smoke. I made my 'assessing an emergency situation' noise, a cross between a choke and scream, and ran to get Mike from the front office.

'Oh shit, the floor,' he said, steely-eyed.

Mike and I came screeching around the corner back into the crematorium. At that same moment, from the chute where the bones are swept out, came a sluice of *gushing molten fat*. Mike pulled out the bone-collecting container, roughly the size of a large shoebox, to find a pool of what had to have been five litres of opaque slop. And it kept coming. And coming. The two of us replaced container after container at the bottom of the bone chute like we were bailing out a leaky boat.

Mike ran the containers to the prep room, washing the fat down the same drain as the blood from the embalming process. Meanwhile I plunked down on the floor with a pile of rags, sopping and swabbing up the fat as it cascaded out.

Mike kept apologising, the first time Mike had apologised for anything in my whole time at the crematorium. Even he was on the verge of heaving after the tenth round of smoke, heat, scrub, swab, repeat.

'It's the floor,' he said, defeated.

'The floor? The beautiful new retort floor?' I said.

'The old floor had all those craters, the fat could pool there and burn up later in the cremation. Now the fat has nowhere to go, so it's gliding out the front door.'

When at last the situation was under control, I looked down to find my dress stained with warm human fat. (Would you call this colour burnt sienna, or is it more of a marigold? I wondered.) I was sweaty, defeated, and drenched in lard, but I felt alive.

Cremation was supposed to be the 'clean' option, bodies sanitised by fire into a pile of inoffensive ashes, but Mrs. Greyhound would not go, as Dylan Thomas said, gentle into that good night. We did not succeed in making her disposal tidy, despite all the tools of the

161

modern death industry, the hundreds of thousands of dollars of industrial machinery. I wasn't sure we should be trying as hard as we were for the perfect death. After all, 'success' meant using all the plastic and wires to present the idealised corpse of Elena Ionescu. 'Success' meant dead bodies taken from their families by professionals whose job was not ritual but obfuscation, hiding the truths of what bodies are and what bodies do. For me, Mrs. Greyhound blew the truth of the matter wide open: Death should be *known*. Known as a difficult mental, physical, and emotional process, respected and feared for what it is.

'Jesus, do you need, like, a dry-cleaning stipend or something?' Mike asked, standing over me.

I cackled helplessly, sitting on the crematorium floor in my fat-stained dress, my legs sprawled in front of me, surrounded by rags. It was a moment of release. 'I think this dress is done, man. You can buy me lunch or something. Fucking hell.'

I was horrified that this had happened to Mrs. Greyhound, but it would be a lie to describe the experience as anything less than exhilarating, the repulsive going hand in hand with the wondrous.

My work at Westwind had given me access

to emotions I didn't know I was capable of. I would start laughing or crying at the drop of a damn hat. Crying at a particularly beautiful sunset or a particularly beautiful parking meter, it didn't matter.

It felt as if my life up to this point was spent living within a tiny range of sensations, rolling back and forth like a pinball. At Westwind that emotional range was blasted apart, allowing for ecstasy and despair like I had never experienced.

Everything I was learning at Westwind I wanted to shout from the rooftops. The daily reminders of death cast each day in more vivid tones. Sometimes in mixed company I would share the story of molten fat or some other cringe-inducing tale from the crematorium. People performed their scandalised reactions but I felt less and less connected to their revulsion. The most salacious stories — bones ground in a metal blender or torture-spike eye caps — had the power to disrupt people's polite complacency about death. Rather than denying the truth, it was a revelation to embrace it, however disgusting it might sometimes be.

Alas, Poor Yorick

There are many words a woman in love longs to hear. 'I'll love you forever, darling,' and 'Will it be a diamond this year?' are two fine examples. But young lovers take note: above all else, the phrase every girl *truly* wants to hear is 'Hi, this is Amy from Science Support; I'm dropping off some heads.'

Westwind had ongoing cremation contracts with two anatomical-donation facilities, of which Science Support was one. Several dozen lucky Californians who donated their bodies to be poked and prodded for the good of scientific enquiry ended their journey in my fiery care.

After the phone call from Amy, a truck crept through the gate at Westwind and pulled up next to the rear entrance where Chris unloaded his daily round of bodies. The back door creaked open. Two young men poked their heads in and looked around suspiciously. 'Uh . . . yes, afternoon ma'am, we're Science Support here with, your uh . . . heads.'

No matter how many times the transport truck came to visit Westwind, the Science Support drivers always looked supremely uncomfortable. They couldn't drop their cargo and get out of the crematorium fast enough. It made me proud to know that the drivers of Ye Olde Travelling Body Parts Truck were intimidated by *my* workplace.

Science Support is essentially a body broker, accepting whole dead bodies for donation and then dividing them up and selling the parts, as a junkyard does for old cars. Science Support isn't the only name in the body-broker game. Several large companies trade in this macabre (but quite legal) field. Or, I should say, quite legal *in the US*. While attending a conference in London, I brought up private, for-profit body donation during a panel. The UK professionals and medical ethicists looked at me like I'd suggested the brutal murder of a kitten. In the UK, your only shot for whole body donation is to a medical school.

There are many positives to donating your body to science. In the modern death landscape, body donation is the only surefire way to make sure your death is free. After your death, Science Support will pick up your corpse, transport you to their facility, use you to cure cancer (note: results may vary), and then pay for your cremation at Westwind.

Indeed, your body might be used on the front lines of medical research. My own grandfather died after a long, debilitating bout with Alzheimer's, including one memorable Christmas Eve where he managed to steal the car keys in the middle of the night and disappear for seven hours into downtown Honolulu. Ho-ho-horrible Christmas morning to you too, family. If the donated heads of Alzheimer's patients, with brains containing the plaques and tangles that turned my grandfather into a stranger, could make a difference to other families, off with their heads, I'd say.

Unfortunately, not every dead body goes to what might be considered 'noble ends.' There is a slim possibility that your donated head will be *the* head, the head that holds the key to the mysteries of the twenty-first century's great disease epidemics. But it is equally possible your body will end up being used to train a new crop of Beverly Hills plastic surgeons in the art of the facelift. Or dumped out of a plane to test parachute technology. Your body is donated to science in a very ... general way. Where your parts go is not up to you.

The use of corpses for the advancement of science has come a long way in the past four hundred years. In the sixteenth century, medicine was practised with a feeble grasp of how the human body actually functioned.

Medical texts misunderstood everything from how blood flowed through the body to the locations of vital organs to what caused sickness to develop in the first place (accepted answer: imbalances in the body's four 'humours' — phlegm, blood, black bile, and yellow bile). Renaissance artist Andreas Vesalius, upset that medical students were learning human anatomy by dissecting dogs, secretly plucked corpses of criminals from the gallows. It wasn't until the eighteenth and nineteenth centuries that surgical training schools consistently provided human anatomical dissections for teaching and research. The demand for corpses was so high that professors took to robbing fresh graves for bodies. Or, in the case of William Burke and William Hare in nineteenth-century Scotland, murdering living people (sixteen of them) and selling their bodies to be dissected by a public anatomical lecturer.

The two men from Science Support rolled a large box off the back of their truck. In the box were two human heads, surrounded by ice packs filled with small gelled beads that resembled Dippin' Dots ice-cream. As soon as I signed for the shipment, the gentlemen slammed shut the back of their truck and screeched out of the parking lot. This exchange was typical. The Science Support fellows regularly brought deliveries of torsos, heads, and other assorted viscera. We also got a single leg once, but that wasn't from Science Support.

'Hey, Caitlin, you see that leg in the reefer?' Mike asked. After six months as his colleague I could discern the subtle distinction between all-business Mike, genuinely asking if I had seen the aforementioned leg, and wry, sarcastic Mike, about to crack the most minuscule of smiles.

'Well, no Mike, I haven't seen this leg you speak of. Is it a Science Support leg?'

'No, man, the lady's alive,' he said. 'She had it amputated yesterday. Diabetes, I guess. She called to see if we could cremate just her leg. That was the weirdest phone call. Chris picked it up at the hospital this morning.'

'She's cremating *just* her leg? So you're telling me this is a . . . premation?' I replied. My joke was rewarded with a hint of a laugh.

'Pre-cremation — premation — that's good. Like the guy we got from San Jose last week. The one who set himself on fire with his cigarette. Premation.' He shook his head and turned back to the computer.

Score one for appropriately timed morbid humour. I had spent months trying to impress Mike with my death-positive gumption, but he was only now beginning to trust me with a joke.

The heads in this Science Support box belonged, respectively, to a gentleman of eighty and a lady of seventy-eight. Each head came with long identification sheets. The sheets didn't give us their names or where they were from, but did provide a whole list of superfluous fun facts like 'Head No. 1 is allergic to shellfish, tomatoes, morphine, and strawberries,' and 'Head No. 2 has brain cancer and is prone to hay fever.'

There is little chance my two heads could have known each other in real life, but I wanted to imagine they were two lovers separated by war. The Crusades, perhaps. The Crusades seemed like a romantic, violence-soaked backdrop for this sort of thing. Maybe they were victims of a single guillotine blade during the French Revolution. Or perhaps the early American frontier — had they been scalped? I pulled back the gel ice packs to peek in. No, no, these heads had their scalps intact. Regardless, here they were, together, on their way to the eternal pyre.

Hesitant, I peeked into the box of heads. I toyed with the idea of not unwrapping them. They could go straight in the cremation machine, right? Mike popped up behind my shoulder, always watching. 'You gotta take those gel packs out; those aren't good for the retort.'

'Won't I have to take the heads out to do that?' I asked.

'Yeah, well, let's see what kind of woman you are,' he replied, arms crossed.

Chris looked up from his task, putting together a cardboard corpse container with a tape gun. All eyes on me. Boxes of heads really brought people together at Westwind.

I gingerly pulled out the man's head (No. 1, allergic to shellfish, tomatoes, morphine, and strawberries). It was squishy, heavier than I expected it to be. Roughly the weight of a bowling ball but far more unruly, thanks to his brain distributing mass unevenly. A person really needed two hands to hold it.

'Alas, poor Yorick!' I proclaimed to my head.

'Aye-aye, Queequeg,' Chris countered. Our literary references for decapitated heads were at the ready, a kind of funeral-industry improv game.

Mike finished us off with a rambling story about Joel-Peter Witkin, the avant-garde artist who procured heads from Mexican morgues and photographed them in elaborate arrangements alongside hermaphrodites and dwarves in mythical costume. Witkin said his desire to create this dark imagery came from witnessing a horrific car accident as a young boy, where a small girl was decapitated, her lifeless head rolling to a stop at his feet. Mike always had to win the prize for esoterica.

I admired people, like Head No. 1 and Head No. 2, who had given up on a traditional funeral and the idea of post-death 'dignity' for the good of research. It was *très moderne*.

Did that mean I was considering such an end for myself? *Au contraire*. I had a violent reaction to the thought of being fragmented in this way. It seemed like a serious loss of control to have my head lying in a box somewhere, the unbridled anonymity, only a number and my shellfish allergy to define me. My mother had always told me that it didn't matter what we did with her dead body: 'Just put me in a bin bag out on the kerb for the trash guys for all I care.' No, Mother. Donating your body to science was certainly noble, but I revolted at the thought of anonymous portions, sections, and parts scattered about town.

Self-control has always been important to me. My grandfather, the man who went on the Alzheimer's-induced joy-ride on Christmas morning, had been a full colonel in the United States Army. He commanded the tank destroyers in the Korean War, learned Farsi and hobnobbed with the Shah of Iran, and spent his later years running Hawai'i's army base. He was a strict man with definite ideas about how men, women, and children (read: me) should behave. All those ideas went to pot at the end of his life, when Alzheimer's made him confused, sad, and socially inappropriate.

The worst part of his disease was the way it eroded his self-control, and since Alzheimer's is in part genetic, it offered daily reminders of how it might someday erode mine as well. Then again, death brings an *inevitable* loss of control. It seemed unfair that I could spend a lifetime making sure I was dressed well and saying all the right things only to end up dead and powerless at the end. Naked on a cold white table, boobs flopped to the side, blood seeping out the side of my mouth, some random funeral-home worker hosing me down.

I, of all people, had no rational reason to be against scientific donation, against the fragmentation of the body. Part of the fear is cultural. The dismemberment of the body prior to a Tibetan Sky Burial is difficult to accept even though, rationally, cremation is just another kind of fragmentation. The cousin of a friend was killed in Afghanistan. There was a brief period of time after the death when his mother received distressing reports that the roadside bomb that killed him had sent his limbs in all directions. She was relieved to discover his body was intact, even though his body was flown home to be placed directly into the cremation chamber, transformed by fire into thousands upon thousands of anonymous chunks of inorganic bone.

Like it or not, some of those bones will be irretrievable from the cracks between the floor and the wall of the cremation machine. The official State of California cremation authorisation acknowledges this phenomenon with the following language:

> The chamber is composed of ceramic or other material which disintegrates slightly during each cremation and the product of that disintegration is commingled with the cremated remains . . . Some residue remains in the cracks and uneven places of the chamber.

In layman's terms: When you're pulled out of the machine post-cremation, some of the machine comes with you — and some of your bones stay behind. 'Commingling,' it's called.

No matter how many times I dragged the mini retort broom across the breaks in the ceramic surface, fragments of each body were lost. Not that I didn't try. I attempted to gather each sliver. The hot air would scorch my face as I stuck my body a little too far into the machine, dislodging trapped bones with the mini broom until the straw bristles melted into a stump.

Once, while sweeping out the cremation machine, a hot bone fragment launched itself out at me. I accidentally stepped on it and burned a hole deep into the rubber sole of my boot. 'Goddammit!' I yelled, and with an involuntary jerk of the knee I kicked the bone in a high arc across the crematorium. It landed somewhere behind a row of gurneys. After five minutes crawling on my hands and knees I found the ember and matched the piece to the bone-shaped hole in my boot. You will be fragmented.

Of course, there are different perspectives on fragmentation. A month later, Mike gave me two (unpaid, mind you) vacation days to attend the wedding of my cousin in Nashville. In typical pre-wedding fashion, a ladies' spa day was scheduled for the afternoon before the ceremony. I was whisked into the massage room, a windowless den of incense and meditation Muzak. The blonde masseuse, soft-spoken and very Southern, began her heavenly dance across my back, making chit-chat as she massaged.

'So what do you do, sweetheart?' she

drawled over the chanting from the speakers.

Do I tell this woman what I do? I wondered. Do I tell her that her magical fingers are kneading muscle knots caused by the hauling of corpses and scraping of bones from giant ovens?

I decided to tell her.

To her credit she didn't skip a beat. 'Well . . . I can tell you that I've got lots of family in West Virginia and they consider all that cremation stuff to be devil's work.'

'Well, what do you think about cremation?' I asked my masseuse.

She deliberated for a second, her hands resting on my back. 'You know, I'm born again.'

Fortunately I was face-down on the massage table, so she couldn't see my eyes flickering back and forth. I was unsure if I was supposed to ask a follow-up question.

There was a long pause before she continued. 'I do believe Jesus will come at the rapture to take the blessed up to heaven. But here's the thing. I know we will need our bodies, but what if I should be swimmin' in the ocean and get myself torn apart by a shark? My body is bobbing around the water and in the shark's stomach, but are you telling me our Saviour can't make me whole again? If his power can heal a shark attack, he can heal a cremation.'

'Heal a cremation,' I repeated. I had never thought of this. 'Well, hypothetically if God can reconfigure decomposed bodies that have passed through the digestive tracts of maggots, I guess He could probably heal a cremation.'

She seemed satisfied with my reply and we spent the rest of the session in silence, pondering the degree to which we would ultimately be fragmented. Her body would await the rapture. My body, I feared, would enjoy no such transcendence.

It wasn't only the inevitability of fragmentation that got to me, it was the way death was inescapable, sweeping over everything in its path. As Publilius Syrus wrote in the first century AD, 'As men, we are all equal in the presence of death.'

In the late Middle Ages, the 'danse macabre,' or dance of the dead, was a popular subject in art. Paintings depicted decomposing corpses with huge grins who arrive to collect the unsuspecting living. The gleeful corpses, made anonymous by putrefaction, wave their hands and stomp their feet as they pull both popes and paupers, kings and blacksmiths into their whirling dance. The images reminded viewers that death was certain: No one escapes. Anonymity awaits.

The Golden Gate Bridge stretches north

from the tip of San Francisco across the Golden Gate Sound to Marin County. The burnished red-orange architectural masterpiece is the most photographed bridge in the world. You can drive across it at any hour, on any day of the year, and there will be happy couples embracing and taking pictures. The bridge also holds the somewhat infamous distinction of being one of the most popular suicide destinations in the world, squaring off against places like the Nanjing Yangtze River Bridge in China and the Aokigahara Forest in Japan in a competition none of the tourist bureaus particularly want to win.

A man or woman jumping off the side of the Golden Gate can expect to hit the water at 75 miles per hour, and count on dying with 98 per cent certainty. The trauma alone kills most jumpers — their ribs shatter and puncture fragile internal organs. If you do manage to survive the fall, you will drown or develop hypothermia unless someone spots you. Bodies are often found after they have been attacked by sharks or infested with crabs. Some bodies are never found at all. Despite the high death rate (or tragically, *because* of it), people come from all over the world to jump off the Golden Gate. Tourists walking along the bridge to catch the sunset over the Bay encounter signs reading:

CRISIS COUNSELING

THERE IS HOPE

MAKE THE CALL

THE CONSEQUENCES OF
JUMPING FROM THIS
BRIDGE ARE FATAL
AND TRAGIC

The Golden Gate Bridge creates a new corpse in this way about every two weeks. One day, after I had been working at Westwind for about seven months without a single jumper, we got two. Death as the great equaliser needs no better example than the two men brought in to Westwind: a twenty-one-year-old homeless man and a forty-five-year-old aerospace engineering executive.

Where the bodies of Golden Gate jumpers wind up after their plummet into the bay depends on what direction the currents carry them. If the waters brought the body south, San Francisco County took possession and sent it off to the overcrowded Medical Examiner's Office in the city. If the currents bore it north, the body belonged to wealthy Marin County, which had a separate Coroner's Office. The aerospace engineer, an actual rocket scientist, could easily have afforded a mansion in Marin County, but he bobbed south. The homeless gentleman, who never had a job, according to his sister, floated north into the wealthy Marin suburbs. The current under the bridge didn't recognise their relative status; it didn't care what helplessness led them to the bridge. The Bay's current fulfilled feminist Camille Paglia's lament: 'Human beings are not nature's favourites. We are merely one of a multitude of species upon which nature indiscriminately exerts its force.'

★　★　★

One afternoon, Chris and I left the crematorium in his white van and drove into Berkeley to pick up Therese Vaughn. Therese died in her own bed at age 102. Therese was born when World War I — *World War I!* — was still years in the future. After returning to Westwind and placing Therese's body in the cooler, I cremated a newborn baby who had lived a mere three hours and six minutes. After cremation, Therese's ashes and the ashes of the baby were identical in appearance, if not in quantity.

Bodies cremated in full, heads donated to science, babies, and some woman's amputated leg all come out looking the same in the end. Sifting through an urn of cremated remains you cannot tell if a person had successes, failures, grandchildren, felonies. 'For you are dust, and to dust you shall return.' As an adult human, your dust is the same as my dust, four to seven pounds of greyish ash and bone.

There is a great deal made in the modern funeral industry about 'personalisation.' This marketing narrative targets the chequebooks of baby boomers and ensures that, for the right price, every death can come with extras — Baltimore Ravens caskets, golf-club-shaped urns, corpse-shrouding blankets with duck-hunting scenes. *Mortuary Management* (the main death-industry trade rag) proclaimed the arrival of Thomas Kinkade airbrushed burial vaults with rainbow-hued pastoral scenes as if they were the second coming of Christ. These products provide the extra touches that say, 'I'm not my neighbour, I'm not the same as the next dead guy, I'm me, I'm unique, I'm remembered!' But why bother with the golf-club urn when time erases even the best of us? On a trip to Westminster Abbey, weaving my way through the numberless glassy-eyed drones clutching their audioguides, I heard a tour guide lecturing to a pack of assembled tourists. 'Sir Isaac Newton is, of course, a famous scientist buried here at the Abbey, but another is Charles Darwin, buried over there in the floor. Right where that gentleman in a blue wind-breaker is walking. There he goes, walking across the body of Charles Darwin.' Sorry Charles, evolutionary theory proves we're the type of species to tromp right over you in our blue windbreakers.

For me, the schmaltzy tchotchkes provided by the funeral home ignite a horror that would shame the swirling corpses of the danse macabre. Not that I didn't understand the impulse for personalisation.

In fact, I had indulged that impulse when I came to Westwind with the naïve idea of someday opening La Belle Mort, a funeral home for the one-of-a-kind, personalised death. But what we needed wasn't more additions to the endless list of merchandise options. Not when we were missing rituals of true significance, rituals involving the body, the family, emotions. Rituals that couldn't be replaced with purchasing power.

Over the months I worked at Westwind, sacks of cremated remains had been piling up on the metal shelf above the tools. They were babies, adults, anatomical parts from Science Support, and the 'extra' bits from the machines — a leftover mixture of just about everyone who passed through our doors. One afternoon, when there were enough sacks to make a trip worthwhile, we prepared the little grey warriors for their non-witnessed sea scattering. The bags of bones, decedents with names like Yuri Hirakawa and Glendora Jones and Timothy Rabinowitz, were stacked into crates, their little twist ties standing at stoic attention. Family members, next of kin, and Science Support paid our mortuary to take the ashes of their loved ones out onto San Francisco Bay and toss them to the winds.

The preparation took me a while. In California there are laws and procedures for scattering remains at sea. One has to check and then double-check each decedent, each Authorisation for Disposition, each Westwind contract, comparing the little numbers on one form to the little numbers on another. At the end I had three full crates containing the indistinguishable remains of thirty-eight former adults, twelve former infants, and nine former anatomical specimens. I was the leader of my own danse macabre.

The crates were ready to be taken out on Westwind's ash-scattering boat the next morning. I dropped the hint to Mike that I should be the one to go. I wanted to be the one who took these people all the way through, picking them up from where they fell to placing them into the fire to releasing them into the sea. Alas, Mike got that job. He had been looking forward to the early morning seaside adventure. Someone had to stay at Westwind, answer the phones, and burn the bodies. That someone was the crematorium operator, the low woman on death's totem pole: me.

Eros and Thanatos

The house I grew up in, on Punalei Place, had a swimming pool where I spent countless hours as a child. During my teenage years, the pool's cleaning pump broke and my childhood hangout gradually turned green, developed a thick layer of vegetation, and became a wildlife habitat for local frogs and ducks. The flora and fauna were pleased to find a fully developed bog in the midst of a normal suburban street.

I'm sure our neighbours were not impressed with the conservation efforts happening over at the ol' Doughty estate. The bog frogs croaked at impossible volumes throughout the night and it was no secret that the Kitasakis, our neighbours across the street, loathed the pair of mallards that occasionally waddled from our pool over to their lawn to defecate. When both ducks turned up dead lying side by side in the street (fed rat poison — my unconfirmed theory), I took their post-mortem portraits and put a silent hex on the Kitasaki family. They moved out the next year, likely driven mad by their sin and the quality of my hex.

When my parents finally repaired the pool

almost fifteen years later, the men who drained it found a thin layer of bones at the bottom: bird, toad, mouse. None of the bones were human, though, meaning my father won a bet. I thought the odds were good we'd find at least two or three of our former neighbours.

In the early days, when our pool still looked like any other pool, the game of choice for the gang of seven-year-old neighbourhood girls was based on *The Little Mermaid*. The Disney film had come out in 1989 and it was our everything. No self-respecting game of make believe could start without strict parameters. 'I'm a mermaid with a shiny purple bra, long green hair, and a pink tail with sparkles. My best friend is a singing octopus,' one of us would announce. If you called dibs on green hair and a pink tail, no one else had better try a similar colour scheme or soon they'd be ostracised from the group and end up crying behind the banana plant.

The entire Disney oeuvre, *The Little Mermaid* in particular, gave me a hopelessly warped understanding of love. For those of you who have not seen it, allow me to sum up the plot (which differs considerably from the Hans Christian Andersen original — more on that later): Ariel is a beautiful young mermaid with an even more beautiful voice. She is obsessed with becoming a human due to her profound love for Prince Eric (a human she has only seen once) and for the detritus of human civilisation (which she collects in her underwater hoarder cave). An evil hag sea witch tells Ariel she can transform her into a human if she gives up her voice and goes silent. Ariel agrees to the bargain and the sea witch splits her mermaid tail into two human legs. Fortunately, even without her voice Prince Eric still falls for Ariel because she's cute, and cute women don't need voices. The evil sea witch tries to keep them apart, but love prevails and Ariel marries the prince and becomes a permanent human. The End.

I expected this is how my love life would proceed, minus the evil sea witch and the wise but sarcastic musical crab. My teen years disabused me of this notion.

As a teenager with morbid proclivities, my only real social outlets in Hawai'i were the gothic and S&M fetish clubs with names like 'Flesh' and 'The Dungeon' that took place on Saturday nights in warehouses down by the airport. My friends and I, all uniform-wearing private-school girls by day, would tell our parents we were having a sleep-over and instead change into black vinyl ball gowns we ordered off the Internet. Then we'd go to the clubs and get tied to iron crosses and publicly flogged amid puffing fog machines. After the clubs closed at two a.m. we'd go into a twenty-four-hour diner called Zippy's, invariably get called 'witches' by some confused late-night patrons, wash off our make-up in the bathroom, and sleep for a few hours in my parents' car. Since I was also on my school's competitive outrigger canoe paddling team, the next morning I would have to peel off the vinyl ball gown and paddle in the open ocean for two hours as dolphins leapt majestically next to our boat. Hawai'i is an interesting place to grow up.

As an American (well, American-ish) child in the late twentieth century, I had no idea that the stories from my beloved Disney movies were pilfered from brutal, macabre European fairy tales by the Brothers Grimm and Hans Christian Andersen. Fairy tales that didn't end with the familiar 'and they lived happily ever after,' but with conclusions like this, from 'The Goose-Girl' by the Brothers Grimm: 'She deserves no better fate than to be stripped entirely naked, and put in a barrel which is studded inside with pointed nails . . . two white horses should be harnessed to it, which will drag her along through one street after another, till she is dead.'

The plot of Danish author Hans Christian

Andersen's original 1836 story 'The Little Mermaid' is, in fact, entirely devoid of tuneful sea animals. In Andersen's story, the young mermaid falls in love with a prince and goes to the sea witch for help. (So far we're on track with the Disney version.) The mermaid is given human legs, but each step is made to feel like sharp knives slicing into her feet. The sea witch, requiring payment for these services, 'cut off the mermaid's tongue, so that she became dumb, and would never again speak or sing.' The bargain is that if our mermaid cannot convince the prince to love her, she will die, turning to sea foam on the water and losing her chance to have an immortal soul. Luckily, the prince does appear enamoured with her, 'and she received permission to sleep at his door, on a velvet cushion.' Because nothing says love like being allowed to sleep in a man's doorway on a dog bed.

The prince, not sold on the silent woman who sleeps outside his door, marries a princess from another kingdom. Having failed to win the love of her human prince, the mermaid knows she will die the morning after the wedding. At the last minute her sisters swoop in and cut off all their hair, trading it to the sea witch for a knife. They give it to her, telling her, 'Before the sun rises you must plunge it into the heart of the prince; when the warm blood falls upon your feet they will grow together again, and form into a fish's tail, and you will be once more a mermaid.' The mermaid can't bring herself to slaughter her beloved prince, so she leaps over the side of the boat to her death. The End. Try selling *that* one as an animated children's film.

This is the version of the story I wish had informed my childhood. Exposing a young child to the realities of love and death is far less dangerous than exposing them to the lie of the happy ending. Children of the Disney princess era grew up with a whitewashed version of reality filled with animal sidekicks and unrealistic expectations. Mythologist Joseph Campbell wisely tells us to scorn the happy ending, 'for the world as we know it, as we have seen it, yields but one ending: death, disintegration, dismemberment, and the crucifixion of our heart with the passing of the forms that we have loved.'

Disintegration and death have never been the most popular endings with the general public. It's far easier to swallow a good old-fashioned love story. So it is with great trepidation that I tell you my own love story, the one that started the day I walked in on Bruce preparing an autopsied body.

189

'Hey Bruce, did you get the clothes the family brought in for Mrs. Gutierrez yesterday?' I asked.

'Oh man, did you *see* that underwear?' He sighed. 'Now, family, your grandma isn't Bettie Page. Don't bring in a G-string.'

'Why would they do that? That's seriously bizarre.'

'People do that shit all the time. The *g* in G-string does not stand for 'grandma,' c'mon.'

Bruce gestured at the young man who lay on the table in front of him. 'This is the guy that Chris picked up at the coroner's today. Overdose or something.'

That was when I noticed that the man who lay on the table did not have a face. He hadn't been decapitated, he just did not have a *face*. The skin from the crown of his head to the bottom of his chin had been pulled down, revealing the vessels and muscles underneath.

'Bruce, why is he like this? What is going on?' I asked, expecting he would lecture me on some kind of flesh-eating, face-rolling disease.

As it turns out, peeling down the face like the lid of a sardine can is quite common. When a medical examiner performs an autopsy, he or she will often remove the brain. An incision is made at the scalp line, and the skin is pulled down so the examiner can open the skull with an oscillating saw. The scalping technique is surprisingly similar to that of the ancient Scythian warriors, who would bring the heads of their enemies to the king to prove their victory before removing the scalp. A good warrior (or medical examiner) might have a whole collection of scalps on his belt.

After removing the brain, the examiner sets the skull cap back on the dead man or woman's head slightly askance, like a jaunty newsboy cap, and rolls the face back into place. It is the job of the funeral home to put Humpty Dumpty back together again. Bruce was having a difficult time of it that day.

'Look, Caitlin, I tell the family I'm a *mortician*, not a *magician*. You understand?' he grumbled, trotting out his favourite joke.

Bruce was trying valiantly to make the skull fit in place, cutting strips off a towel to prop up the man's forehead. He was frustrated because the supply cupboard in the West-wind preparation room was never stocked with the proper forehead-repair materials.

'Well, what do you need, Bruce?' I enquired.

'Some peanut butter.'

He didn't need actual peanut butter. What he needed was a type of restorative putty that the old-timers in the funeral industry *call* peanut butter. I didn't understand this distinction and spent the next several weeks telling anyone who would listen that morticians spread peanut butter inside our heads as a post-mortem beauty remedy. Choosy embalmers choose Jif peanut butter.

The removal of the young man's face revealed the wide, menacing smile of his skull. It was unnerving to think this same deranged grin lurks just beneath the flesh of everyone's face, the frowning, the crying, even the dying. The skull seemed to know that Bruce didn't need peanut butter, like, you know, *peanut butter* peanut butter. It watched my face screw up in confusion and laughed at my ignorance.

Bruce gently rolled the skin up like a Halloween mask. Voilà, there he was. My stomach dropped down to somewhere below my knees. With the face set back in place I recognised him. The body belonged to Luke, one of my closest friends, his thick brown hair matted with blood.

The day I found out I had got the job at Westwind, Luke, who had never thought my relationship with death was strange, was the first person I told. In his presence I was safe to share my apprehensions about death and life. Our conversations slid easily from the bigger existential questions to slapstick jokes from the British comedies we streamed (ahem, illegally) online. Luke was hysterical, but he was also a listener, a man versed in the art of a well-placed question. Most important, as the months at Westwind wore on and everything I knew about death changed, he understood my doubts and all-too-frequent failures, and never judged me for them.

After an excruciating moment I realised it wasn't *really* him. 'Peanut butter' wasn't really peanut butter and this deceased drug addict wasn't really Luke, who lived hundreds of miles south in Los Angeles. But this man looked shockingly like him, and once seen, the image could not be unseen.

After Bruce had embalmed this pseudo-Luke and gone home for the day, Mike asked me to clean up the body. He lay in the prep room under a white sheet, all sewn back together like a patchwork quilt. I pulled back the sheet to reveal the body and used a warm cloth to wipe the blood from his hair and eyelashes and the backs of his delicate hands. The real Luke was not dead, but now I understood he could die, and I would regret it deeply if my beloved friend died without knowing how vital he was to me.

The psychoanalyst Otto Rank declared modern love a religious problem. As we grow increasingly secular and move away from the towns where we were born, we can no longer use religion or community to confirm our meaning in the world, so we seize a love partner instead, someone to distract us from the fact of our animal existence. French existentialist Albert Camus said it best: 'Ah, *mon cher*, for anyone who is alone, without God and without a master, the weight of days is dreadful.'

On the day I saw Faux Luke in the crematorium I was alone, having moved to San Francisco not knowing a soul. The morning of my twenty-fourth birthday I walked to my car and found a single flower tucked under the windshield wiper. I experienced a moment of euphoria, thinking that someone had remembered. This was followed by a deep sadness when I realised it wasn't possible; there was no one in San Francisco who would have known. Perhaps the wind had brought it there.

After I came home from work that night I bought a pizza and ate it alone. My mother called to wish me happy birthday.

The only other people I saw regularly, other than Mike, Chris, and Bruce, were a group of teenagers. In addition to my nine to five at the funeral home, I moonlighted as an English and history tutor for wealthy high-schoolers in Marin County (recently described by the *New York Times* as being 'the most beautiful, bucolic, privileged, liberal, hippie-dippie place on the earth'). My students were innocent kids with manicured lawns and well-meaning helicopter parents who performed backflips to avoid hearing the details of my day job. Often I would go straight from Westwind in Oakland across the San Rafael Bridge to various mansions overlooking the Bay. It was the only way I could live off my body-burning salary while living in San Francisco.

It was a double life I lived, shuttling between the worlds of the living and the dead. The transition was so abrupt that some days I wondered if they could see it in my eyes. 'Good afternoon, here I am in your multimillion-dollar home covered in people dust and smelling vaguely of rot. Please pay me a large sum of money to mould the impressionable mind of your teenager.' If the parents noticed the dust covering my body, they were kind enough not to mention it. People! It's made of people.

When you know that death is coming for you, the thought inspires you to be ambitious, to apologise to old enemies, call your grandparents, work less, travel more, learn Russian, take up knitting. Fall in love. I decided the moment I saw his doppelgänger lying on the table that what I felt for Luke was love. My feelings were strong, more intense than I had ever experienced. The heavens struck me with their clichéd bolt of lightning. Luke became my ideal, and I desperately hoped he would bring me security and relief from the emotions that had assaulted me over the past months. If I could be with him, I wouldn't die alone; someone would plan *my* funeral and hold my hand and wipe the bloody purge from my dying mouth. I wouldn't be like Yvette Vickers, the B-movie actress and star of *Attack of the 50 Foot Woman*, who was found completely mummified in her Los Angeles home more than a year after her death. She had been a recluse while alive; no one had bothered to check on her. Instead of worrying that my own cat would end up eating my dead body to survive, I projected my loneliness onto Luke.

I was still thinking about Luke when I cremated Maureen. She was in her mid-fifties, diagnosed with a lightning-fast cancer and dead in a little over a year. Maureen left behind a husband, Matthew. By all rights, Matthew should have been the first to go. He was wheelchair-bound and unable to leave his home; Chris had to drive to his apartment to make the arrangements for Maureen's cremation. Written on the wall calendar in big, tragic letters was 'September 17th: Maureen Dies.'

I was the one who delivered Maureen's cremated remains to Matthew's apartment. He wheeled himself down to the lobby, a man with long greying hair and a small, strange voice. As I handed him Maureen's ashes he didn't move, or even look up. He just thanked me in his thin voice, and cradled the brown box in his lap like a child.

✱ ✱ ✱

Fast-forward to Monday morning, and who turns up in our fridge at the crematorium but Matthew. Dead. Given up. His sister came by the mortuary with a small bag of personal items that Matthew had wanted to be cremated with.

Relatives of the deceased asked us to do this all the time. As long as there's nothing explosive among the objects, we're happy to include them; the items just burn up with the corpse. After loading Matthew onto the mechanical belt to place him in the cremation chamber, I opened the bag to empty its contents alongside him. Inside were a lock of Maureen's hair, their wedding rings, and maybe fifteen photographs. Not photographs of the brittle, wheelchair-bound man I had met, but a healthy young man and his blushing bride. Maureen and Matthew: happy, young, beautiful, married over twenty years. They had friends, dogs, what looked like an incredible amount of fun. And each other.

One more item slipped out of the bag. It was the metal identification tag from Maureen's cremation, the one I had burned with her just a few weeks before. These tags stay with the body through the whole cremation, and leave stuck in with the ashes, which is how sacks of cremated remains found in old storage lockers and attics can still be identified years later. The tag I found was identical (except for the ID number) to the one I was putting in with Matthew now. I imagined his hands sinking into the grey mulch of Maureen's bones and finding the tag. I imagined him pulling the tag out and brushing the dusty metal against his cheek. It was a bizarre honour to have been a part of their private last moment together, the last act of their love story.

I cried (sobbed, if we're being honest) standing over Matthew's body, moments before it was loaded into the chamber. Even if all we love will die, I still ached for a love like theirs, to be adored so completely. Had not Disney guaranteed all of us such an ending?

In the fourteenth century Dom Pedro, the heir to the Portuguese throne, fell in love with a noblewoman, Inês Pérez de Castro. Unfortunately, Dom Pedro already had a wife, meaning his affair with Inês was carried out in secret. Several years later, Dom Pedro's first wife died, freeing him to be with Inês at last. Dom Pedro and Inês had several children together, children who were perceived as a threat to the rule of Pedro's father, the king. While Pedro was away, the king had Inês and her children executed.

Furious, Pedro revolted against his father, eventually taking the throne. He ordered Inês's executioners brought back from Castile and had their hearts ripped from their chests as he watched. He declared that Inês was his legal wife and instructed that she be disinterred, some six years after her death. Here, legend mixes with reality, but it is said that Inês was placed on her throne, a crown set upon her skull, and the members of the king's court made to kiss the skeletal hand of their rightful queen.

King Dom Pedro longed for Inês; I longed for Luke. The Portuguese have a word with no equivalent in English, *saudade*, which indicates a longing, tinged with nostalgia, madness, and sickness over something you have lost. The ghastly image of Luke's face detached from his skull was a preview of his death; at any moment, he might disappear. I needed him now, for tomorrow is not promised. But I was willing to play the long game. No matter how long it took, I had to figure out a way to be with him.

Bubblating

The day started innocently enough. 'Caitlin!' Mike hollered from the preparation room, 'Hey, come in here and help me get this big guy on the table.'

Actually, I remember him saying, 'Hey, come in here and help me get this big *Mexican* on the table.' But that cannot be right. Mike was always politically correct in his terminology. (He once referred to the victims of Oakland's gang violence as 'young urban men of colour.') I have trouble believing 'this big Mexican' is not just a trick of my memory. Regardless, the man we transferred from the stretcher to the prep table was neither big nor Mexican. He was massive and El Salvadorian, an insurance salesman who weighed over thirty-two stones. Should you ever wish to understand the phrase 'dead weight' in all its gravitational glory, attempt to lift the corpse of a morbidly obese man off of a perilous, wobbly stretcher.

Juan Santos died from an overdose of cocaine. His body went undiscovered for two days in his apartment in the East Bay. He was autopsied by the medical examiner and his chest sewn back up leaving a dramatic Y-shaped stitch stretching from his clavicle to his stomach. 'Did you catch this guy's bag of viscera in the back of the reefer?' Mike asked.

'Viscera? All his organs and stuff?'

'Yeah, the medical examiner takes the organs out and piles them in those red hazardous material bags. Comes in to the funeral home with the body.'

'Just, like, tucked up next to 'em or something?' I asked.

Mike grinned. 'No, Chris carries them slung over his shoulder like Santa Claus.'

'Really?'

'No, man, no. What the hell — that's gross,' Mike said.

Ah, Mike in a jovial mood. I tried to play along with his Yuletide-themed organ humour. 'So that's where the legend of 'Chris' Kringle comes from? Is it the good or bad kids that get internal organs for Christmas?'

'I guess it depends on how morbid a kid you are.'

'Does it all get put back in the body?'

'Eventually. When Bruce comes in this afternoon to embalm him. There's a service tomorrow, so he'll soak them in embalming sludge and stick them back in,' he explained.

After hoisting Juan onto the table with a theatrical heave, Mike brought out a tape measure. 'The family bought a casket, too. I'm going to measure him. I hope he fits because I *really* don't want to call this family back and tell them they need the oversized casket. Maybe I'll make you do it,' Mike said, smiling at the thought.

The World Health Organisation (along with any of the forty-five extreme-weight-loss television programmes) tells us that the United States has more overweight adults than any other country in the world. It's no surprise that the market for oversized caskets is booming.

The website for Goliath Casket, Inc. features this charming origin story:

Back in the 1970's and '80's oversize caskets were hard to get and poorly made. In 1985, Keith's father, Forrest Davis (Pee Wee), quit his job as a welder in a casket factory and said, 'Boys, I'm gonna go home and build oversize caskets that you would be proud to put your mother in.' . . . The company started in an old converted hog barn on their farm, by offering just two sizes and one colour.

We could have used Pee Wee's ingenuity, because there was no way Juan was going to fit into a regular-sized casket. The man, bless his departed soul, was almost as wide as he was tall. 'Go ahead, cross his arms, like he's in the casket,' Mike instructed.

I stretched myself across Juan's body to access both appendages. 'No, cross them harder, harder, harder,' Mike insisted, extending the tape measure across his shoulders. By now I was fully spread out over the body. 'Keep going, keep — there we are! Boom. He will totally fit.'

'Oh, c'mon, he will not!' I said.

'We'll make him fit. The family is already paying more than they can afford for this service. I'm not going to tack on the extra $300 for an oversized casket if I can help it. Just telling them their son *needs* an oversized casket is hard enough.'

Later that day, as the Cremulator whirred through the backlog of bones, Bruce arrived to embalm Juan. After seeing him laid out, Bruce, always one for tact, yelled into the crematorium: 'Caitlin! Caitlin, this is a lot of Mexican. It's gonna stink. Bigger people always stink.'

'Why does everyone keep calling him Mexican?' I yelled back over the rumble of the cremation machines.

Bruce was wrong about Juan's country of origin, and surely he was also wrong about fat people stinking. Yet emanating from the preparation room was the most ferocious smell my nostrils e'er had smell'd. You would think such an odour would have repelled me, but for some reason it aroused a desire in me to find the pot of gold at the end of the olfactory rainbow.

I had seen Bruce embalm bodies, but I was in no way intellectually or emotionally prepared to see thirty-two stones laid out before me. Autopsied bodies require the embalmer to cut open the stiches from the Y-shaped incision and, as Mike had said, to chemically treat the deceased's internal organs from Santa Chris's red hazmat bag. Bruce had just begun that portion of the preparation when I walked in.

To describe the scene as a 'swampy mire' simply would not do it justice. It was more guts and blood and organs and fat than I could ever have imagined a single human body containing. Bruce, who was pulling the organs out of the bag, launched into a narrative immediately: 'I told you it would stink, Caitlin. Bigger people just decompose faster. That's science, girl. It's the fat; the bacteria *love* the fat. By the time they get here after going in for an autopsy, phew.'

To Bruce's credit, this turned out to be true. His 'bigger people always stink' comment wasn't based on prejudice, it was a fact.

'All that stuff is bubblating in that body. I call it bubblating. At least this guy didn't die in the tub. Tubs are the worst. The *worst*. You go to take a body out of the tub and the skin just pulls right off. The tissue gas bubbles up, all oily, and *the smell*.' Bruce whistled for dramatic effect. 'Psychologically, you'll be smelling that for the rest of the day, rest of your life sometimes.'

He kept on talking. 'Look at this guy. Cocaine overdose? More likely he had a heart attack. Look at this,' Bruce said as he reached into Juan's chest cavity, picked up his heart, and presented it to me. 'Look at his heart! All this fat around it. You know he was sittin' there with his friends at the bar eating a hamburger and doin' his lines of coke. All this stuff' — he pulled his gloved hands apart to reveal the yellowed deposits — 'this is why you can't be fat!'

I must have looked insulted at this accusation, because he quickly added, 'Naw, I don't mean *you* specifically can't be fat, girl, you got a good figure. But I know you must have fat friends. Tell your fat friends.'

I had no reply.

For Bruce, the former instructor, this demonstration was not done for shock value, but for the benefit of my education. Obese people smell particularly bad after an autopsy

206

due to their faster rate of decomposition. Fact. Not that we would ever share this fact with a decedent's family. You couldn't have paid me any sum of money to explain to Juan's mother the truth about why her son smelled the way he did. These facts were only for the ears of the deathmongers, the initiated behind the scenes.

Much of our negative reaction to a decomposing corpse like Juan's is raw instinct. We've evolved to be disgusted by things that would hurt us to eat, rotting meat being one of the top contenders in that category. Some animals, like vultures, can safely consume rotting flesh because of their highly corrosive stomach acid. But humans would prefer to avoid spoiled food altogether rather than having to fight off the ill-effects after the meat has entered our bodies. Recall the Wari', consuming their decomposing brethren and being forced to leave the ritual, have a bit of a vomit, and return to eat again.

'Bruce, seriously Bruce,' I said. 'This might be the worst thing I have ever smelled.'

For those of you who have not had the privilege of smelling Eau de Decomposition, the first note of a putrefying human body is of licorice with a strong citrus undertone. Not a fresh, summer citrus, mind you — more like a can of orange-scented industrial bathroom spray shot directly up your nose. Add to that a day-old glass of white wine that has begun to attract flies. Top it off with a bucket of fish left in the sun. That, my friends, is what human decomposition smells like.

Bruce was apologetic. 'Yeah, I'd tell you not to smell it, but that would be like tellin' a little kid, 'Son, don't you dare push the big red button!''

Except for the rare decedent like Juan Santos who slips past the system, decomposition and decay have all but disappeared from our way of death. The modern corpse has two options: burial with preservative embalming, which grinds decomposition to a halt into perpetuity (or at least until the body starts to harden and shrivel like a mummy); and cremation, which turns the body into ash and dust. Either way, you will never see a human being decaying.

Because we've never encountered a decomposing body, we can only assume they are out to get us. It is no wonder there is a cultural fascination with zombies. They are public enemy number one, taboo extraordinaire, the most gruesome thing there is — a reanimated decomposing corpse.

There is a misconception that 'burial' involves placing a body directly into the earth, leaving us vulnerable should the zombie apocalypse come about. Like in Michael Jackson's 'Thriller' video, a decayed hand shoots up through the dirt and the body hops easily out of its grave. Burial in that fashion *used* to be the case, but in the developed world the paradigm no longer fits. Instead, a body is chemically embalmed, then laid in a sealed casket, which is then placed in a heavy concrete or metal vault beneath the earth, surrounding the body in several layers of artificial embrace, separating it from the world above. The headstone is placed on top of the whole affair, like the cherry on a death-denial sundae.

Vaults and caskets are not the law; they are the policy of individual cemeteries. Vaults prevent the settling of the dirt around the body, thus making landscaping more uniform and cost effective. As an added bonus, vaults can be customised and sold at a markup. Faux marble? Bronze? Take your pick, family.

Rather than let author and environmentalist Edward Abbey be buried in a traditional cemetery, his friends stole his body, wrapped it in a sleeping bag, and hauled it in the back of his pickup truck to the Cabeza Prieta Desert in Arizona. They drove down a long dirt road and dug a hole when they reached the end of it, marking Abbey's name on a nearby stone and pouring whiskey onto the grave. Fitting tribute for Abbey, who spent his career warning humanity of the harm in separating ourselves from nature. 'If my decomposing carcass helps nourish the roots of a juniper tree or the wings of a vulture — that is immortality enough for me. And as much as anyone deserves,' he once said.

Left to their own devices, human bodies rot, decompose, come apart, and sink gloriously back into the earth from whence they came. Using embalming and heavy protective caskets to stop this process is a desperate attempt to stave off the inevitable, and demonstrates our clear terror of decomposition. The death industry markets caskets and embalming under the rubric of helping bodies look 'natural,' but our current death customs are as natural as training majestic creatures like bears and elephants to dance in cute little outfits, or erecting replicas of the Eiffel Tower and Venetian canals in the middle of the harsh American desert.

Western culture didn't always have this aversion to decomposition. In fact, our relationship to rot used to be altogether *intimate*. In the early days of Christianity, when the religion was still a small Jewish sect fighting for its survival, those who worshipped the new messiah faced harsh persecution, sometimes dying for their faith. These martyrs came to grisly ends. You had your beheadings, your stonings, your flayings, your crucifixions, your hangings, your boilings in oil, your eatings by lion, and so forth. As a reward, the martyrs went straight to heaven. No purgatory, no Judgement Day: just a direct shot into the kingdom of God.

For medieval Christians, these martyrs-cum-saints were celebrities. When the emperor Constantine declared Christianity legal in 324 AD, the bodies of martyred saints became major attractions. Having the dead body of a famous martyr in your church — or even just a heart, bone, or vial of blood — brought hordes of worshippers. It was believed that the souls of the saints lurked around their corpses, dispensing miracles and general holiness to those who came to pay tribute.

Diseases were cured! Droughts were ended! Enemies were defeated! But why stop at just paying a visit to a dead saint when you could be buried in the same church? It stood to reason that being buried for all eternity *ad sanctos* (literally 'at the saints') would ingratiate you to the saint in the afterlife, ensuring protection for your immortal soul.

As the Christian faith grew, more and more members of the congregation insisted on being buried in and around the church to reap the benefits of saint proximity. This burial practice spread throughout the empire, from Rome to Byzantium and to what is now present-day England and France. Entire towns grew up around these corpse churches.

Demand rose and the churches supplied it — for a fee, of course. The wealthiest church patrons wanted the best spots, nearest the saints. If there was a nook in the church big enough for a corpse, you were sure to find a body in it. There were, without hyperbole, dead bodies everywhere. The preferred locations were the half circle around the apse and the vestibule at the entrance. Beyond those key positions, it was a free-for-all: corpses were placed under the slabs on the floor, in the roof, under the eaves, even piled into the walls themselves. Going to church meant the corpses in the walls outnumbered the living parishioners.

Without refrigeration, in the heat of the summer months, the noxious smell of human decomposition in these churches must have been unimaginable. Italian physician Bernardino Ramazzini complained that 'there are so many tombs in the church, and they are so often opened that this abominable smell is too often unmistakable. However much they fumigate the sacred edifices with incense, myrrh, and other aromatic odours, it is obviously very injurious to those present.'

If you weren't rich or influential enough to score a spot inside the church, you would go into one of many graves in the church's courtyard, some pits thirty feet deep, containing up to 1,500 corpses. This practice reflected a seismic shift from the pre-medieval Roman and Jewish belief that dead bodies were impure, and best kept on the far outskirts of town. The medieval church courtyard turned cemetery was *the* place to see and be seen. It was the centre of town life, a place of socialisation and commerce. Vendors sold beer and wine to the crowds and installed communal ovens to bake fresh bread. Young lovers took nightly strolls; speeches were made to gathered crowds. The Council of Rouen in 1231 banned dancing in the cemetery or in the church, under pain of excommunication. To require such a forceful ban, it must have been a popular pastime. The cemetery was the venue where the living and the dead mingled in social harmony.

Historian Philippe Ariès, author of a brilliant, sweeping study of a millennium of Western death entitled *L'homme devant la mort*, declared that 'henceforth and for a long time to come, the dead completely ceased to inspire fear.' Ariès may have been exaggerating, but even if the Europeans of the Middle

Ages were afraid of death, they got over it, because the sublime benefits of being near the saints outweighed the drawbacks of living with unseemly sights and smells.

Medieval death was my first true (academic) love. I was captivated by the dancing skeletons, the maggot tomb décor, the charnel houses, the putrefying bodies in the church walls. The brazen acceptance of human decomposition in the late Middle Ages was so different from what I grew up with. The only two funerals I had been to as a child were Papa Aquino's, with his heavily embalmed and made-up face sneering up from his casket, and the memorial service for a mother of a childhood friend. Her body was absent from the service altogether, and instead of speaking directly of her death, the pastor running the memorial spoke only in euphemisms: 'Her soul was a tent, and the cruel winds of life came through the palm trees and blew our sister's tent down!'

Decomposition was rare even behind the scenes at Westwind. At ye olde warehouse of modern secular death, the majority of our clients died in contained medical environments like nursing homes or hospitals before being swiftly whisked away to our cold-storage fridge, which, while not freezing, maintained a steady temperature below 4.4°C. Even if the bodies had to hang out there for a few days while the proper state permits were filed, most corpses were cremated *long* before they ever made it to the smellier phases of decomposition. One morning I came in, opened the freezer door, pushed aside the plastic strips, and was blasted by the unmistakable, unforgettable smell of human decomposition.

'Chris, dear God man, why? Who is it that smells like that?' I asked.

'His name is Royce, I think. Picked him up yesterday. It's not good in there, Cat,' Chris answered, shaking his head with a seriousness I appreciated. This vile, corrosive smell was indeed no laughing matter.

So it is you, Royce, source of the horrible, infernal stench emanating from the fridge. I worked my little fingers to the quick to file his death certificate with the city so I could then cremate him as quickly as possible. When I opened his cremation container, I found a man who could best be described as 'boggy.' Royce was vivid green, like the colour of a 1950s Cadillac. He was a 'floater,' the unfortunate funeral-industry term for bodies found dead in the water — in Royce's case, the San Francisco Bay. I sent him to the flames, satisfied that my day of decay had come to an end.

But the smell did not go away. Royce was gone — and yet — the smell persisted. This matter required investigation. Investigation of the worst possible kind. Sifting through the cardboard boxes of bodies sniffing away until . . . *You!* — Ellen! The woman from the Medical Examiner's Office. 'Tis, in fact, *you* who stinks more putridly than the worst smelling thing ever to smell. You, with your skin flaking away. What happened to you? You were fifty-six and your death certificate says you worked in 'fashion sales.'

Unlike Royce, who had floated in the Bay for several days, I never found out what had happened to Ellen. When at last I was able to send the poor woman to the pyre, I sat down and read a chapter of Octave Mirbeau's *The Torture Garden*, a book I first encountered during my decadent French literature phase. Not three lines into the chapter a character was described as 'a lusty dilettante who revelled in the stench of decomposition.' My first reaction was, 'Lovely, just like me!' But really? No. *Not* just like me, not like anyone who worked at Westwind. It may have been an academic interest, but that didn't mean I took some perverse, maniacal delight in decomposition. I didn't walk into the fridge every day, inhale deeply, and cackle with delight, dancing around naked in the cold miasma, transgressing with obscene pleasure. Instead, I wrinkled my nose, shuddered, and washed my hands for the twelfth time that day. Decomposition was just another reality of death, a necessary visual (and aromatic) reminder that our bodies are fallible, mere blips on the radar of the vast universe.

That reminder of our fallibility is beneficial, and there is much to be gained by bringing back responsible exposure to decomposition. Historically, Buddhist monks hoping to detach themselves from lust and curb their desire for permanence would meditate on the form of a rotting corpse. Known as the nine cemetery contemplations, the meditation would focus on the different stages of decomposition: '(1) distension (*choso*); (2) rupture (*kaiso*); (3) exudation of blood (*ketsuzuso*); (4) putrefaction (*noranso*); (5) discolouration and desiccation (*seioso*); (6) consumption by animals and birds (*lanso*); (7) dismemberment (*sanso*); (8) bones (*kosso*); and (9) parched to dust (*shoso*).'

The meditation could be internal, but often the monks employed images of the stages of decay or took trips to the charnel grounds to meditate over a real decomposing corpse. There is nothing like consistent exposure to dead bodies to remove the trepidation attached to dead bodies.

If decomposing bodies have disappeared from culture (which they have), but those same decomposing bodies are needed to alleviate the fear of death (which they are), what happens to a culture where all decomposition is removed? We don't need to hypothesise: we live in just such a culture. A culture of death denial.

This denial takes many forms. Our obsession with youth, the creams and chemicals and detoxifying diets pushed by those who would sell the idea that the natural aging of our bodies is grotesque. Spending over $100 billion a year on anti-aging products as 3.1 million children under five starve to death. The denial manifests in our technology and buildings, which create the illusion that we have less in common with road kill than with the sleek lines of a MacBook.

The way to break the cycle and avoid embalming, the casket, the heavy vault, is something called green, or natural, burial. Or perhaps most delightful, although this term is only used in the UK: woodland burial, which calls to mind all manner of precious forest creatures acting as cemetery caretakers. It is only available in certain cemeteries, but its popularity is growing as society continues to demand it. Natural burial is what transpired with Edward Abbey's remains, minus the whole stealing-the-corpse-and-hightailing-it-into-the-desert thing. The body goes straight into the ground, in a simple biodegradable shroud, with a rock to mark the location. It zips merrily through decomposition, shooting its atoms back into the universe to create new life. Not only is natural burial by far the most ecologically sound way to perish, it doubles down on the fear of fragmentation and loss of control. Making the choice to be naturally buried says, 'Not only am I aware that I'm a helpless, fragmented mass of organic matter, I celebrate it. Vive la decay!'

By this stage of my time at Westwind, I had already decided on a green burial for my own body. I understood that I had been given my atoms, the ones that made up my heart and toenails and kidneys and brain, on a kind of universal loan programme. The time would come when I would have to give the atoms back, and I didn't want to attempt to hold on to them through the chemical preservation of my future corpse. There was one such natural burial cemetery in Marin, right across the bridge from Westwind. There, I could sit among the cemetery's rolling hills, looking down over the mounded graves and contemplate my date with decay. The monks found liberation through their discomfort, and in a way I was doing the same. Staring directly into the heart of my fear, something I could never do as a child, and ever so gradually, starting to break clear of it.

Ghusl

The Buddha — of Buddhism fame — was born Siddhartha Gautama in what is now Nepal. Young Siddhartha was not born enlightened; he spent the first twenty-nine years of his life ensconced in palatial luxury. Siddhartha's father, the king, had been warned that his son would grow into a great spiritual thinker if he came into contact with suffering or death. Naturally, his father preferred Siddhartha end up a king like him, rather than a measly thinker, so he banned death of any kind within the palace walls.

When Siddhartha reached twenty-nine he announced his desire to explore the surrounding city. His father agreed but arranged things so that his son saw only young, healthy people engaging in young, healthy-people activities. But the gods were having none of that: they sent an old man with grey hair, missing teeth, and a limp to surprise Siddhartha, who had never before seen old age. Siddhartha next saw a man infected with plague and finally, the pièce de résistance, a corpse burning on a wooden plank. Having confronted old age, sickness, death, and nothingness all in one trip, Siddhartha renounced palace life and became a monk. The rest, as they say, is religious history.

In the Siddhartha story, the crude physicality of the burning corpse is not a negative force but a positive one. It catalysed his transformation. Encountering a corpse forced the man who would be Buddha to see life as a process of unpredictable and constant change. It was life *without* corpses, trapped behind the palace walls, that had prevented him from reaching enlightenment.

Westwind Cremation & Burial changed my understanding of death. Less than a year after donning my corpse-coloured glasses, I went from thinking it was strange that we don't see dead bodies any more to believing their absence was a root cause of major problems in the modern world.

Corpses keep the living tethered to reality. I had lived my entire life up until I began working at Westwind relatively corpse-free. Now I had access to scores of them — stacked in the crematorium freezer. They forced me to face my own death and the deaths of those I loved. No matter how much technology may become our master, it takes only a human corpse to toss the anchor off that boat and pull us back down to the firm knowledge that we are glorified animals that eat and shit and are doomed to die. We are all just future corpses.

Jeremy, the body on the prep room table today, was a fifty-three-year-old man covered in tattoos. Half of his life had been spent in prison. Many of his tattoos were self-inked and had faded into a dull green. Numbers and letters dotted his arms, torso, and back. Jeremy also had tattoos that were brand-new, from his time post-prison. They were colourful images of birds and waves and other metaphors for freedom. He left prison and sought liberation in a new, different life. The tattoos were stunning. The concept of the body as canvas becomes more powerful if the canvas is dead.

As I started to wash Jeremy, the bell at Westwind's front gate rang. I pulled off my gloves and headed into the courtyard. Before I could even muster a 'Hello, come in,' a woman, who subsequently introduced herself as Jeremy's sister, squealed, 'Hey there, six-footer!'

'Oh yes, well, I'm pretty tall, you're righ — '

'My, my, my, what a big, beautiful girl you are!' she shrieked, wrapping me in a huge hug. I thanked her, even though her saying 'big, beautiful girl' gave me flashbacks to Bruce explaining that deposits around the heart were the reason I shouldn't be fat.

I showed Jeremy's sister into our arrangement room, where she pulled out a lollipop and began grinding it down with her teeth while furiously tapping her foot. I didn't want to make assumptions, but if pressed I might have guessed she was high on some manner of amphetamine. She would not have been the first family member I had spoken to in such a condition, the burden of selling low-cost funeral services in Oakland.

'Honey, here's what we're going to do,' she said. 'I want a nice funeral for Jeremy in San Francisco, then he's gonna be buried at the veterans' cemetery in Sac Valley. I'm gonna drive behind you all the way.' The cadence of her speech synched up with the tapping of her foot.

'You're aware the cemetery is two hours away?' I said.

'Y'all are gonna cremate him if I don't keep an eye on you. I can't be sure you didn't do it already.'

'Ma'am, the veterans' cemetery is expecting the body to arrive in its casket for burial. We're going to deliver it there on Thursday,' I explained.

'You're not listening. That's what I'm saying; his body isn't in any casket, *you cremated him without my permission.*'

I tried to explain in the nicest way possible that it made no logistical or financial sense for Westwind to cremate Jeremy and then deliver an empty casket to the Sacramento Valley National Cemetery, but she wasn't buying it.

Jeremy's sister wasn't the only one who assumed we death workers were up to no good. People had wild theories about what we did with the bodies. Elderly women would call the crematorium, their voices shaky and slightly confused.

'Westwind Cremation and Burial, this is Caitlin,' I would answer.

'Hello, dear, I'm Estelle,' said one woman. 'You are going to cremate me when I die. I have the paperwork with your company and it's all paid for. But I saw a thing on the news this morning about you all burning the bodies together dear, is that right?'

'No, no ma'am, everyone is cremated on their own here,' I said firmly.

'They said you put a pile of bodies on a bonfire and there is a big pile of ashes afterwards and you just scoop from that pile,' Estelle said.

'Ma'am, I'm not sure who 'they' are.'

'The news people,' she said.

'Well, I promise they aren't talking about us here at Westwind. Everyone gets their own serial number and is cremated alone,' I assured her.

She sighed. 'Well, OK dear. I've lived so long and I'm just real afraid about dying and being left in a pile of bodies.'

Estelle wasn't alone in her fears. One woman called to ask if bodies were kept hanging on meat hooks in the refrigerator like sides of beef. An enraged gentleman informed me we shouldn't be charging for a sea scattering because all that meant was 'dumpin' the ashes in the toilet with a packet of salt and flushing.'

It broke my heart to hear them, even the ones who were screaming at me. Holy crap, you've been *thinking* that? I thought. You think you're going to die and be hung on a meat hook before being thrown into a bonfire of corpses and flushed down the toilet?

Hearing these fears took me back to being eight years old and believing spitting into my shirt was keeping my mother alive. I began to experiment with complete honesty. Everyone who asked these sorts of questions got brutally clear answers. If they asked about how the bones became ash, I'd say, 'Well, there's this machine called the Cremulator . . . ' If they asked whether their body would rot before cremation, I'd say, 'See, the bacteria start eating you from the inside out as soon as you die, but body refrigeration really puts a stop to that.' The strange thing was, the more honest I was, the more satisfied and grateful people were.

Holding a witness cremation — though it gave me palpitations — solved many of these problems. People saw what was actually happening — saw the body, saw it glide into the cremation retort alone, even symbolically took part in the process by pushing the button to start the flames. The retort may have been a huge machine opening its mouth to eat your dead mother, but pushing the button offered a participatory ritual nonetheless.

I felt a growing compulsion to do more, to change how the public understood death and the death industry. There was an admirable group of women in the Bay Area working towards this change, who performed funerals at the dead person's home, referring to themselves as Death Midwives or Death Doulas. They had not been trained or licensed by the funeral industry but saw themselves as New Agey vestiges of a time past, when the body was taken care of by the family.

Prior to the Civil War, as previously mentioned, death and dying were strongly associated with the home. 'Home is where the corpse is,' they would say. (They didn't say that, I made it up, but they might as well have said it.) Since corpses were a domestic affair, the duty to care for them fell to women. Women baked the meat pies, did the laundry, washed the corpses.

In many ways, women are death's natural companions. Every time a woman gives birth, she is creating not only a life, but also a death. Samuel Beckett wrote that women 'give birth astride of a grave.' Mother Nature is indeed a real *mother*, creating and destroying in a constant loop.

If the matriarch of your family didn't want to wash and shroud the body herself, the family could hire 'layers-out of the dead.' In the early nineteenth century it was mostly women who had this job, a tradition brought over to the American colonies from England, where it had long been the accepted practice. There were midwives for babies and layers-out for corpses; women to bring you into the world and women to take you out of it.

Most of Westwind's clients didn't realise the dead body was theirs to take care of as they wished. They didn't have to hand Dad over to a funeral home, or even hire a death midwife. That body, for better or worse, belonged to them. Not only was caring for your own dead legal in California (as it is in most of the Western world), dead bodies are far from the nefarious creatures the modern death industry has made them out to be. In Muslim communities, it is considered a 'meritorious deed' to wash and shroud the dead in a ritual washing known as Ghusl. The person who performs the Ghusl is chosen by the dying man or woman themselves. Men are washed by men and women are washed by women. Selection is an honour and a sacred obligation to fulfill.

Though the 'layers-out of the dead' were an import from England, the modern English death system can be a horror for the family who wishes to be more involved postmortem. If a person dies in a hospital, there are viewing rooms for the family to come visit the body, which sounds like an excellent service. Unfortunately, the trauma of the death is compounded by the uncomfortable isolation of the viewing room. The family is taken out of the modern, well-appointed hospital, and guided through a dark hallway with peeling paint and dripping pipes and yellow waste bins, the same corridor used by hospital catering and laundry departments. They are ushered into a tiny room with two chairs and the corpse, awkwardly secluded from the rest of the hospital. One viewing room was even outside in a shed. It is only recently that there has been a movement in some hospitals to modernise the viewing rooms with inviting colours and lighting.

In centuries past, before society fully understood bacteria and germs, outbreaks of disease, from cholera to the Black Death, were believed to originate from 'bad air' floating like a mist off corpses. Larger cities took to burying their dead far outside city limits. While it's true that bodies create offensive sights and smells, a dead human body poses very little threat to a living one — the bacteria involved in decomposition are not the same bacteria that cause disease.

A few weeks before my encounter with tattooed Jeremy and his sister, Westwind received a visit from Miss Nakazawa, a young woman whose mother had died at home. She wanted to keep her mother's body in the house for a few more hours after she died to say her good-byes, but she said, 'The police detective told me I had to call you guys right away because she had diabetes and keeping the body any longer might harm my family.'

'I'm sorry, ma'am, he told you what?' I replied, my jaw on the floor.

'He told me we had to have a mortuary come pick her up right away or the body will make us sick.'

To recap: a police detective thought this family was going to be harmed by diabetes caught from a dead body. He might as well have told her she was going to get AIDS from a toilet seat. Putting aside the misguided idea that someone can 'catch' diabetes from another person, much less a corpse, most viruses and bacteria, even those that *could* potentially cause disease, only live for a few additional hours in a dead body. The rare virus that survives longer (for example, HIV, up to sixteen days under refrigeration) poses no more harm in a dead body than in a living body. It's more dangerous to your health to fly on an aeroplane than it is to be in the same room as a corpse.

Miss Nakazawa had contacted another funeral home before Westwind, but was told her mother absolutely had to be embalmed if the family wanted to see her again. 'We don't want Mom embalmed,' she said. 'She was a Buddhist and didn't want that, but the funeral director told me we had to embalm the body for health reasons.'

Great. So two 'professionals' in one day told this woman that her dead mother was a ticking time bomb of highly hazardous deadness that was going to infect her whole family. Embalmers embalm because they think it makes the corpse look better, because they've been told it's what's 'right' and 'decent,' and because it makes it easier to control the viewing. Also, they get paid for it. Not because the microorganisms present in an un-embalmed body pose any threat to a family. Now that we have a sophisticated understanding of germ theory and the science of death, police detectives and funeral professionals have no excuse for saying that proximity to the dead will harm the living.

Because of superstition, unquestioned even among those who should know better, this woman wasn't given the opportunity to sit with her mother until, as a friend of mine put it, her grieving 'felt . . . done, somehow.' She missed her chance for closure. A corpse doesn't need you to remember it. In fact, it doesn't need anything any more — it's more than happy to lie there and rot away. It is *you* who needs the corpse. Looking at the body you understand the person is gone, no longer an active player in the game of life. Looking at the body you see yourself, and you know that you, too, will die. The visual is a call to self-awareness. It is the beginning of wisdom.

When a death occurs on the Indonesian island of Java, the whole town is obligated to attend the funeral. The body is stripped of clothing, the jaw closed with a cloth tied around the head, and the arms crossed over the chest. Close relatives of the deceased wash the body, holding the corpse on their laps, positioned so the living are soaked in the water as well. The idea of cradling the dead this way, according to anthropologist Clifford Geertz, 'is called being *tegel* — able to do something odious, abominable, and horrible without flinching, to stick it out despite an inward fear and revulsion.' The mourners perform this ritual to become *iklas*, detached from the pain. Embracing and washing the corpse allows them to face their discomfort head-on, and move to a place where 'their hearts are already free.'

Even if she didn't realise it, this is the type of closure Jeremy's sister wanted as well. After she left Westwind, at last convinced Jeremy's body hadn't been cremated on the sly, I stood over him in the prep room. I read the story his tattoos told and forced out of my head the uneasy voice that had narrated my rookie months at Westwind, suggesting that perhaps his hand would rise up and seize mine, keeping me forever on edge. Nor did I worry that I was somehow going to mishandle or break his body. I thought instead of what his tattoos meant, and about how some people would look at this man and judge him as dirty, a criminal.

He *had* been a criminal, but he was also beautiful. I wasn't there to judge, only to make him clean and dress him in his powder-blue polyester suit with the ruffled tuxedo shirt. Holding up his arm to wash it, I paused: I was *comfortable*. I wanted other people to know that they could do this too. The washing, the comfort. This confident, stable feeling was available to anyone, if society could overcome the burden of superstition.

Ten months into my job at Westwind, I knew death was the life for me. I wanted to teach people to take care of their own dead like our ancestors used to. Washing the corpse themselves. Taking firm control of their fear. Several options presented themselves. The first was to pack my bags and steal away in the night, leaving the crematorium to join the death midwives. This would mean abandoning the funeral industry and the security and legitimacy (deserved or not) it provided. I didn't mind leaving behind the commercialism and up-selling parts of the industry. The problem was, as a general rule, the midwives were far more, shall we say, *spiritual* than I was. I had no moral objection to sacred oils, incense, and death chakras, but as much as I respected these women, I did not want to pretend death was a 'transition' when I really thought of it as, well, a death. Done. *Finito*. Secular to a fault.

My second option was to attend mortuary

school, but that meant going even deeper into the industry and all its ghastly practices.

'You know you don't need to go to mortuary school, Caitlin,' Mike told me. 'Why would you put yourself through that?'

Mike had not gone to mortuary school himself, the fortunate beneficiary of a California state law that doesn't require classwork to become a licensed funeral director. A degree in *anything* (looking at you, BA in basket weaving), a lack of felonies, and a passing score on a single test, and you're in the club.

But now that I had embraced my calling as a mortician, I wanted to know everything, understand everything. I could run to the fringes or I could go back to school for another degree, learn how to embalm, and see first-hand what they were teaching. As much as the death midwives' practices appealed to me, I didn't want to throw pebbles at an iron fortress. I wanted to be on the inside. I decided to apply to mortuary school. Just in case.

Solo Witness

It was November when Mike took a two-week fishing vacation with his wife and child, leaving me — deer-in-the-headlights *me* — in charge of the crematorium. Worse yet, Mike had scheduled a witness cremation for first thing Monday morning. With him gone, I would have to perform the dreaded witness by myself.

'Dear God, Mike, reiterate all procedures and dispense positive reinforcement immediately!' I pleaded.

Mike took a different approach: 'Don't worry, man, it's a real nice family. From New Zealand. Or Australia? Whatever, the son is cool, and I think he's straight. He likes *Six Feet Under*, so there you go. Try to look nice on Monday. He's coming into like twenty pieces of property. I'm trying to set you up.'

It was the beginning of a Jane Austen novel, if Mr. Darcy was a grieving son/HBO enthusiast from Perth and Elizabeth an entry-level cremationist.

Disaster lurked around every corner during a witness cremation. Just a few weeks earlier, the conveyor belt that's used to roll the body into the cremation retort had developed a problem with its electrical system. The short caused the belt to stall occasionally. The stall was not much of an issue if I was alone; I could solve the problem by taking a running start and ramming the cardboard body box into the retort. But if the conveyor belt stalled during a witness, that option seemed far less viable.

I practised what I would say if the worst occurred: *Oh, yes, that conveyor always stops right there. This is the part where I take a sprint across the crematorium and slam myself into the box containing your mother and shoot her into the flames. Common procedure, sir; worry not.*

The night before the witness I had nightmares about the conveyor belt breaking or, worse, the machine turning off as I loaded in the body. That had never happened before, but theoretically it *could — and with my luck would —* happen that day.

As another bit of fodder for my nightmares (besides telling me he wanted to set me up with the deceased's son), the only other information Mike had given me was 'Heads up: she's not looking so good.' The whole family was flying in from New Zealand (slash maybe Australia) and the deceased was 'not looking so good.' What did that even *mean*?

What it meant, as I discovered Monday morning, was that Mother's cheeks had developed strange patches of bright-orange rot and her nose was covered with a hard brown crust. Her face was puffy and smooth, like an overripe peach. Human skin is confined to a dull colour palette of cream, beige, taupe, and brown when people are alive, but all bets are off once someone is dead. Decomposition allows skin to flower into vivid pastels and neons. This woman happened to be orange.

As soon as I arrived at work I started on her make-up. I used whatever was available in Westwind's make-up kit — half special mortuary make-up, half bottles from the drugstore down the street. I tried primping her hair to distract from the decomposition. I placed white sheets around her face, which was the size (and colour) of a basketball, in an attempt at a flattering angle. After rolling her under the rose-coloured lamplight of the viewing room, she didn't look half bad.

'Not too shabby, Cat. Not bad,' Chris reassured me. 'She was looking . . . unwell.'

'Thanks, Chris.'

'Look, I gotta pick up Mr. Clemons from the nursing home on Shattuck. They don't hold bodies for anything; the nurse has already called squawking three times.'

'Chris, there's a witness right now. I'm the only one here!'

'I know, I know, I don't agree with it either. Mike shouldn't have left you like this. He thinks everything's easy. You need backup.'

True as this might have been, my old 'Nope, got it' reflex kicked in. The fear of looking weak or incompetent was worse than any make-believe disaster involving stalled conveyor belts or orange skin.

'Go, Chris. It's fine. I got it.'

Shortly after Chris's departure, the woman's son (Mike's dream date for yours truly) showed up with ten family members in tow. I escorted them into the viewing room and led them over to the body. 'I'll leave you alone with her. Take all the time you need,' I said, backing respectfully out of the room.

As soon as doors were shut, I put my ear up next to the wood, anxious to hear their reaction. The first thing the son said, quite emphatically, was, 'She looked better before. Mom looked much better before all this make-up.'

My immediate instinct was to fling the doors open and yell, 'You mean when she was visibly decaying, buddy?' but I was aware that wasn't the best customer-service move. After I had calmed down and overcome the insult to my handiwork, I wanted to speak with the son again, to tell him that I didn't agree with the corpse-make-up industrial complex either, that natural *was* better, but that *maybe* if he had seen her he would have agreed the make-up was warranted. Then I would ask him to clarify what he meant by 'she looked better before.' Was 'before' when she was still alive? That made sense. Or was 'before' when he last saw his mother and she wasn't yet the colour of a traffic cone? Most unsettling of all was the possibility that he was one of the rare creatures genuinely comfortable with bodies that have already moved into the stages of decomposition. In which case Mike was right, maybe this guy was my dream man. Either way, the conversation never happened and I'm pretty sure our rom-com relationship was doomed, despite the excellent meet-cute premise.

The family took their time viewing their matriarch before coming to get me for the cremation. Back in the chapel I was alarmed to find smoke wafting out from the sides of the corpse. The family had laid several thick bundles of burning sage in the folds of her white sheets. We didn't usually allow open fire in the viewing room, but since Mike was gone and Mom resembled sports equipment, I let it slide.

Along with the incense, the family had placed a Häagen-Dazs coffee-and-almond ice-cream bar between her hands like a Viking warrior's weapon. Those are my favourite. So I yelled, involuntarily, 'Those are my favourite!'

I had successfully kept my mouth shut up till that moment (even after the insult to my skills as a corpse beautician), but ice-cream proved a topic on which I could not remain silent. Thankfully, they just laughed. Coffee ice-cream bars were their mother's favourite too.

With Chris retrieving Mr. Clemons, it was up to me to transfer Mom into the crematorium. My first act was to ram the cot firmly into the doorframe, spewing forth a burst of sage smoke. I don't remember exactly what I said — mortification clouds the memory — but it was probably something along the lines of 'Whoops!' or 'First door's always a doozy!'

I lifted Mom onto the conveyor belt without incident, and then, to my relief, the belt's soothing whir accompanied her right into the cremation machine. I let her son push the button to start the flames. Like many before him, he was moved by the button's ritual power. The incense and ice-cream had shown that this family was no stranger to ritual. For the moment it seemed he had forgotten the rammed door and the theatrical make-up (though he still wasn't charmed enough to ask me out).

While Mike was on vacation, I cremated twenty-seven adults, six babies, and two anatomical torsos. Three of those cremations were witnessed, and they went off without a hitch.

On his first morning back, Mike glanced up from his paperwork and said, 'I'm so fucking proud of you.'

I almost burst into tears right there. I felt like I had conquered something huge, like I was no longer a girl playing dress-up at this job. I wasn't a dilettante. I was a crematorium operator. It was something I knew how to do. It was a skill. And I was good at it.

If Mike had been in the habit of flattering my vanity the way I'd hoped he would, congratulating me on a well-swept courtyard or my cremating five babies before five, I would have become a far less competent worker. I succeeded because I needed to prove myself to him.

'You've stepped it up more than 95 per cent of the people we've hired, man,' Mike continued.

'Wait, who are the 5 per cent who worked harder than me?' My eyes narrowed. 'That had better just be an expression.'

'We usually have to hire people with no experience. Or, if they do have any experience they're goons from the removal service. I mean, it's kind of a disgusting job.'

'That doesn't pay very much,' I added.

'No,' he said with a laugh, 'it doesn't. We tricked you into it.'

My excitement at finally squeezing legitimate praise from Mike was short-lived, promptly turning into guilt. I had applied to mortuary school, and had been accepted.

Being accepted didn't mean I had to attend. This was the end of 2008, the beginning of the economic crisis, a foolish time to quit any stable job, even a job as bizarre as crematorium operator. But my life in San Francisco was still bland and lonely, and the Cypress College of Mortuary Science (one of only two mortuary schools in California) was located in Orange County, the suburban wonderland just south of Los Angeles and home to the *Real Housewives* and Disneyland. I didn't want to be an embalmer, the trade taught at mortuary schools like Cypress, but I did want to discover first-hand how our national mortality racket was training its future members. Where, exactly, did things go so wrong: with the people who ran the industry, the people who taught them, or the industry itself?

Then there was Luke, more of a consideration than I would then admit to myself, who had been living in Southern California for several years. At the end of college we had planned to move to Los Angeles together, to get an apartment, and to live as penniless but fulfilled artists. Instead I broke north for San Francisco and pursued my wild hare of a death obsession. It was a selfish decision at the time, but things were different now. I knew who I was, my life had a purpose, and I was ready to be with him.

'So, you're moving to L.A., Doughty? For real this time?' Luke asked, sceptical.

'Don't be too flattered, buddy. It's not that I want to move to L.A., per se, I just have to get away from all these corpses. Have you read *Explosion in a Cathedral*?

'I am tired of dwelling amongst the dead . . . Everything smells of corpses here. I want to return to the world of the living, where people believe in something.'

He laughed. 'Everything smells of corpses, eh? What's your metaphor with that? Is the crematorium made of corpses?'

'Yes, but they are incredibly difficult to build with,' I explained.

'I thought they were pretty stiff.'

'Right, so good for initial bracing. But their constant decay is bad for foundational security. Unpredictable, you know?'

'Caitlin, I think you should get out of there before all of those corpses come crashing down around you.'

Luke tipped the scales. I would head south for the winter.

I finally told Mike a week later. He kept a poker face and said, 'Well, if that's your decision.'

It was more obvious that Chris didn't want me to go. We had memories together, like the time we picked up an elderly hoarder lying in a pool of her own blood on the kitchen floor, the counter cluttered with open peanut butter and Nutella containers crawling with cockroaches. Many of our memories were disgusting, but they were our memories nonetheless.

As my departure approached, we posted the opening for my job on the Internet, and people applied in droves. The job market must have been abysmal, because people seemed eager to work in a mortuary.

Many people were applying to the job listing, but that didn't mean many *good* people were applying to the listing. From one cover letter: 'You can trust me because I am a Muslim. I don't do fraud. There could be a $100 bill on the floor and I would not pick it up. The one thing that motivates me is incentive: If I run 3 miles a day, what will I get?'

Then there were the myriad applications with incorrect spelling/terminology/grammar: 'Objective: To aquire experience and gain oppurtunity to work in field of mortuary.'

The real gems came in when we selected several people to fill out an additional questionnaire. I thought that the questionnaire was a little much, in an 'if you were a tree what kind of tree would you be?' way, but one has to separate the wheat from the chaff.

Q: In approximately 300 words explain why you are interested in working at a mortuary.

A: I love the death.

Q: Are you aware of, or have you participated in any religious/spiritual rituals surrounding death? Please describe these events.

A: I play with the wigy [sic] board once.

Q: Are you able to be empathetic to people without becoming personally involved? Describe a situation where you were able to do this.

A: I kill a bunch of people once.

Q: Are you able to be flexible with regards to your job duties and description?

A: Oh hell yeah.

These candidates' qualifications aside, Mike eventually hired Jerry, a tall, attractive African American man. Ironically, Jerry had previously worked for the removal service. He was one of the removal 'goons' Mike swore up and down he would never hire just a few weeks earlier. I guess when your other candidate's experience is having played 'with the wigy board once,' it shifts your perspective.

The week before I left, Chris's clunker of a white van was in the shop. I made the mistake of referring to his much loved van as such. 'Clunker? Young lady, don't insult her integrity. She's been with me for twenty years,' he said. 'She's my Great White Whale, the beast that drags down careless men.'

I dropped Chris off at his parents' home. The house was high up in the Berkeley Hills, where his family has lived since the 1950s. 'Cat, I want to show you something,' he said, leading me to the base of a tree in the centre of the front yard. It was a coastal redwood, maybe fifty feet tall and twenty feet around.

'My mother died when I was really young, so I spent a lot of time with my grandmother. After my mom died, Grandma gave me one of these leaves and told me that if I planted it in the ground a tree would grow from it. It sounded ridiculous, but I planted the leaf in a

Maxwell House coffee container and gave it three cups of water every morning. And here she is,' he said, lovingly patting the base of the tree. 'This is my tree. If you ask me what my greatest accomplishment in this world is — well, here you have it.'

He continued: 'Of course, it's so big now that the roots are starting to push into the neighbour's driveway. Any day now she's going to call the city and have them come tear out everything that's on her property and the whole tree will die. Rot and collapse. I have nightmares about that.'

So much for sentimentality.

To my surprise, the staff at Westwind held a party in honour of my departure. Everyone was there. Chris, who didn't much care for parties, left early, but not before giving me a plastic party bag covered in pastel balloons. The only thing inside was a dried-up coconut.

'It's . . . a coconut? Thanks, Chris.'

'In 1974, when I was living in Hawai'i, my friend threw that coconut into the backseat of my orange Pinto. He said, 'That's an important coconut. Keep it, and take it with you wherever you go.' So I did. And now I'm giving it to you.'

Leave it to Chris to imbue a thirty-five-year-old coconut in a party bag with profundity. I was touched. I gave him an awkward hug.

'Bye, Cat,' he said, and walked out.

Later that evening, when I was about two and a half sheets to the wind, Mike and Bruce got me into a conversation about work. (None of us really had much to talk about apart from work.) But this wasn't the usual chit-chat about the asshole who worked at a competing crematorium or the difficult case last week, it was about the existential stuff, the stuff I had wanted to talk about for so long.

Bruce told the story of an arrangement he had made with a pregnant woman ten years earlier. She had told him the arrangement was for her baby. 'When she came in I said to her, 'That's a shame about your baby, but you're lucky you're pregnant, and gonna have another child.' But the baby she was making arrangements for was the baby in her stomach. It had died and they couldn't take it out yet. That baby was eight months old. That tripped me out. She's sitting in front of me with a dead baby in her. That was messed up. All these years I remember that. To this day, man. That's why there's so many alcoholics and drug addicts in the mortuary business, so you can forget about what's going on.'

Mike leaned his head against the wall, not

looking at me directly. Then, sincerely, as if he really wanted an answer, he asked, 'Aren't there times when the sadness gets to you?'

'Well, I — '

'When the family is so sad and lost, and you can't do anything to help them?'

I thought I saw tears in his eyes. It was dark. I can't be sure. Mike was human after all — another soul coping with the strange, hidden world of death, trying to do his job and figure out what it all meant.

As desperate as I had been for someone to talk to about these very things, in the moment all I could do was mumble, 'I guess so. It is what it is, right?'

'Sure it is. Good luck in L.A.,' he said.

And with that, my career at Westwind Cremation & Burial came to an end.

The Redwoods

The last night I spent on Rondel Place, our landlord — the gay Catholic Filipino vegetarian activist (and collector of angel figurines) who lived in the apartment above us — called the cops on two gentlemen who had stumbled out of Esta Noche in the wee hours of the morning. After urinating on the walls they came to sit on our stoop to smoke and grope each other while whispering fervent Spanish nothings.

Their whispers turned to screams, '*¿Por qué no me amas?*' which turned to vicious blows. The law had to intervene.

Early the next morning, after my night of live-action telenovela, I drove away from Rondel Place in a rented van, carrying all my worldly possessions. Together with my cat and my python, our motley crew made the six-hour journey south from San Francisco to Los Angeles.

Luke had asked me to stay at his place while I searched for an apartment. It was painful to even be in his presence, so overwhelming was my desire to divulge the way I felt about him. Afraid that these feelings would upset the delicate balance of our relationship, I declined his offer and quickly settled in Koreatown. Several people had warned me that Koreatown was a 'bad neighbourhood,' but after living on Rondel Place, it seemed like heaven. I could walk down the street without once encountering a naked man defecating behind my car or a woman in a full intergalactic space-clown costume smoking a crack pipe. There may have been some light drug deals and gang violence on Catalina Street, but in comparison to Rondel Place it was a verdant oasis.

In Los Angeles, I plunged headlong into research on death and culture — not only how it affected our behaviour but *why*. Death practice was a calling, and I followed it with an earnestness that my cynical nature would have never allowed before. Having a purpose was nothing short of exhilarating.

But for every bit of exhilaration, my emotions would also swing to the opposite end of the spectrum. I believed so intensely in the importance of death ritual that I worried it might come across as morbid or pathological. Worse still was the fear of isolation — I was a leader in the cult of the corpse, but so far there was no one else at the temple. A cult leader alone in his beliefs is just a crazy dude with a beard.

But I did have Luke. He represented the comfortable place where I could escape the bonds of death and crawl into the blissful distraction of love. Or so I thought.

I finally lived in the same city as Luke, but I still couldn't speak the words to him directly — they were too loaded. When I could stand it no longer, I wrote him a letter telling him how much I needed him, how his support was the only thing keeping me together in a world where it was all too easy to hand yourself over to despair. The letter was equal parts sappy and nihilistic. Fitting, I thought, as Luke and I were both equal parts sappy and nihilistic. I left it for him in his mailbox in the middle of the night. I felt sure that he was expecting this, and that his response would be as ardent as my declaration.

And then — silence.

After several days, I received a single-line e-mail from Luke:

Don't ask me for this. I can't see you again.

Somewhere in the world, Luke was technically alive. But the relationship I knew, the friendship I cherished, crumbled to dust before my eyes. It was a type of death, and the pain was acute. It didn't take long for my mind to start up the old standby, my running inner monologue. Some sections were similar to the voice of my childhood: *People out there are starving, dying for real. This one guy doesn't want you, well boo-de-hoo, dumb bitch.* And new material was added to the script: *You thought you could escape, didn't you? Well, you can't. You belong to death now, and no one can love someone like that. Everything smells of corpses here.*

★ ★ ★

My job at Westwind lasted until the end of November, and mortuary school didn't begin until January; in between, I felt aimless. I drove up to the far north of California to hike through the giant redwood trees, intending to get my mind off of what had happened with Luke. I wrote my friends (and my mother) a lighthearted e-mail detailing what I wanted done with my body (and my cat) were I to perish on the winding mountain roads.

I checked into the Redwood Hostel, an old house along the jagged Northern California coast. The next day I set off to find the Cathedral Trees Trail, where I had hiked several years before, but for some reason I couldn't find it. I drove up and down the highway, unable to locate the entrance. Suddenly my frustration gave way to rage, and I slammed my foot all the way down on the accelerator and drove full-speed towards the edge of a cliff, swinging the wheel at the very last moment to avoid driving off. Pulling off to the shoulder to catch my breath, I marvelled at my own fury. I wasn't prone to outbursts of violence. I had certainly never tried to drive off a cliff before.

After collecting myself, I stopped to ask directions from a park ranger, who led me to the turn-off for the Cathedral Trees Trail. There was no one on the trail with me as I descended into the canopy of towering, sacred trees, some more than a thousand years old. I could sense their ancient wisdom as I made my way down the hill. It was when I reached the bottom that I realised I had gone there to die. I hadn't consciously planned to do so, but I had written my last e-mails, stated what I wanted done with my body, and carried with me in my backpack the agent of my demise. Twenty minutes earlier I sped straight towards the cliff's edge because I was furious at myself for being so pathetically lost, ruining the sanctity of my final day.

I felt fucking cheated. Culture exists to provide answers to the big human questions: love and death. When I was still a young girl, my culture made me two promises. The first promise was that society knows what's best for us, and what's best for us is that death be kept hidden. That promise was shattered at Westwind, which I had discovered was playing its part in a vast mortality cover-up. Now that I had seen our society's structural denial of death, it was hard for me to stop thinking about. I wanted to quiet my brain, to stop its incessant ruminations on the whys and hows of mortality. I felt like Muchukunda, the mythical Hindu king who, when asked by a god what reward he desired for his years of fighting (literal) demons, wished for nothing more than never-ending sleep. Death, for me, was like a never-ending sleep. And I longed for it.

The second promise was delivered by popular culture, which laid out the narrative that a girl is owed the prize of true love. I didn't believe myself to be a slave to popular-culture narratives (spoiler: I was). Instead I believed what I shared with Luke was a rational, passionate connection with another human being. But somehow I was wrong about everything. Both of the promises my culture made to me were broken, my webs of significance snapped. None of my privileged assumptions about the world could be counted on any more.

For what seemed like hours, no one came

by. This was a well-trodden hiking trail, but today there was absolutely not a soul. So there I sat, debating whether or not to walk into the forest. If I did, I would follow the example of painter Paul Gauguin, who tried to commit suicide by swallowing arsenic deep in the mountains of Tahiti. He had just finished one of his greatest paintings, *Where Do We Come From? What Are We? Where Are We Going?* Gauguin hoped that no humans would find his body so that ants would eat his corpse. In his zeal, he swallowed *too much* arsenic. His body rejected the poison, and he vomited it back up. He woke up, wandered out of the mountains, and lived for six more years.

Like Gauguin, I wanted the animals to devour my body. There is, after all, a thin line between a corpse and a carcass. I was just as much an animal as the other creatures in the redwood forest. A deer needs no embalming, sealed caskets, or headstones. He is free to lie where he dies. My whole life I had eaten other animals, and now I would offer myself to them. Nature would at last have its chance with me.

Botflies can smell a carcass from ten miles away. Chances are they would arrive first to the feast. They would lay their eggs on the outside of my corpse, eggs that would need only a single day to hatch into maggots. The new maggots would tunnel into my body, impervious to the onset of my putrefaction. A marvel of engineering, their mouths allow them to breathe and eat at the same time.

If you are interested in the other, more honourable, guests at the feast, may I submit the bald eagle, symbol of America? They are natural scavengers and do not pass up the opportunity to take advantage of dead meat. Their sharp beaks would rip away strips of my flesh and carry them into the sky.

My body in the woods might also attract a black bear. Omnivorous, they can hunt fish and even young moose, but they have no compunction about scavenging dead bodies. One of which I would become.

After the animals had consumed my flesh, the dermestid beetle would be the final creature to arrive. These plain, inconspicuous beetles eat wool, feathers, fur, and, in my case, dried skin and hair. They would eat everything except my bones, leaving my bare, white skeleton lying anonymously on the forest floor.

In this way my body's decomposition would also be a banquet. My corpse would not be a disgusting mass of corruption but a source of life, dispensing molecules and creating new creatures. It would be the finest acknowledgement that I was but one tiny cog in the ecosystem's wheel, a blip in the majestic workings of the natural world.

We all know how this story turned out. In spite of my fear of living, I chose not to die.

I had become a lonely creature in my time at Westwind, but like Chris held on to thirty-five-year-old coconuts, I held on to friends. These friends didn't live in San Francisco or L.A., but they were out there, along with my parents, who loved me desperately. I didn't take much stock in the value of my life in that moment, but I knew I didn't want them to feel the hopeless ambiguity I had felt years before, left to guess what had become of the little girl at the shopping mall.

I walked out of the forest, and turned the corner into a magnificent field of wildflowers. The colours were brighter than I thought colours could be.

Walking out of the redwoods into the parking lot, somewhat stunned, I ran into a woman, the first person I had seen in hours. She asked for directions. 'My husband always handled that sort of thing,' she apologised. 'He died last year. Sometimes I don't know what to do with myself.'

We talked for some time about death, the cremation process, and our culture's negative relationship with mortality. At her request, I described what had happened to his body at the crematorium. 'Knowing all that stuff makes me feel better,' she said with a smile. 'I don't know why, but it does. I'm glad I met you.'

The only other car in the parking lot was a beat-up old van, filled to the brim with canned food and supplies. Its owner, a rotund woman, walked her black Pomeranian on a nearby patch of grass.

'That's a darling dog,' I said as I climbed into my car.

'So, you think this one is cute, do you?' she croaked.

She walked to the side of her van and returned with two Pomeranian puppies, a gold one and a black one, two perfect balls of fluff. She thrust them into my arms.

That evening, I wandered back to the Redwoods Hostel, dazed and drained by the day, Pomeranian puppy spittle on my cheek from where they had licked my face. On the porch was a tall, handsome nineteen-year-old named Casey, hitchhiking across Canada and down the West Coast of the United States.

Two days later he was at my apartment in Koreatown, lying beside me in my bed, just young and uncomplicated enough to relieve the turmoil in my brain.

'Dude, I could really mow down on some

pasta or something right now,' he mused.

'Yeah, that can be arranged.'

'Seriously, this is, like, crazy, right? I never expected to meet some random awesome chick like this.'

Well, Casey, expect anything. The only thing that's certain is that nothing ever is.

Deth Skool

A week before I started classes at Cypress College of Mortuary Science, I was poked, prodded, and shot up with tetanus and tuberculosis vaccines — all part of the orientation programme. I was sick, which the doctor at the clinic found wildly unimpressive. 'Well, your nodes aren't swollen,' he said. Well, thank you for your opinion, Doctor, I thought. You're not the one taking your mortuary school ID photo looking like a bog monster.

All the disease testing and immunisations caught me off guard. Westwind Cremation had never seemed too concerned with the possibility of me giving syphilis to a corpse or vice versa. The only time Mike would tell me to put on any biohazard protection beyond a pair of rubber gloves was when he thought I might ruin a nice dress. A rare area of sensitivity for him, really.

The morning of my first day of school I left my apartment in Koreatown early and drove the forty-five minutes south to Orange County. I hadn't budgeted for the gridlock traffic in the school parking lot, so of course I was five minutes late. I burst in just as the head of the programme was explaining how tardiness of any kind would be counted as an absence.

'And where exactly are you supposed to be?' he asked as I bumbled in.

'Well, I'm pretty sure I'm supposed to be here,' I replied, slinking to a seat in the back.

There had been a mortuary-school group orientation session a few weeks earlier, which I had missed in order to indulge my despair in the redwoods. This was the first time I was able to see the people I would be spending the next eighteen months with. Looking around the room I was surprised to discover that most of my fellow classmates were women, and women of colour, no less. Hardly the bastion of creepy white men in suits I associated with the American funeral industry.

At the end of our first day we were corralled into a large room with the second- and third-semester students and given instructions to introduce ourselves and tell the group why we had come to the illustrious concrete halls of deth skool. I was hoping this sharing exercise would help ferret out my fellow death revolutionaries. Surely they would boldly refuse to give the same cheesy, party-line answer, 'I just really want to help people.'

No such luck. Even the students with the

crazy eyes, the ones you could just tell enjoyed the transgressive proximity to dead bodies, *had* to talk about their desire to help people. Finally the sharing circle arrived at me. I imagined myself yelling, 'A new dawn is upon us, join me while you still can, fools!' Instead I said something about having worked at a crematorium and, you know, seeing a 'good future in the death industry.' Then it was over. Everyone grabbed their *Nightmare Before Christmas* messenger bags and left in a thoughtful mood.

There were roughly fifty of us starting the programme. I quickly befriended Paola, a first-generation Colombian American. One woman I did not have the pleasure of befriending was Michelle McGee. Nick-named 'Bombshell,' her image was later plastered all over the media for her role in breaking up the marriage of America's sweetheart Sandra Bullock and her tattooed husband Jesse James, a tabloid dream of a cheating scandal. Michelle dropped out two weeks into the programme. It may have been the fact that her whole body was covered in tattoos, including her face (not the traditional look a family is expecting when choosing someone to look after their deceased mother). Michelle was the first to go, but others followed at an alarming rate.

One thing that was immediately apparent about the professors at Cypress College of Mortuary Science was that they *believed* in the work they were doing. Professor Diaz, a short blonde woman, was the most aggressively cheerful person I had ever met in my life. Her enthusiasm for embalming, caskets, and all the available swag of the modern funeral industry bordered on the threatening. In her lectures she described embalming as an ancient art and said things like, 'Do we have to embalm our bodies? No, but we do. *It is who we are.*'

In one class, Professor Diaz showed us lengthy slide-shows of different caskets, gushing over her own purchase of a $25,000 Batesville Gold Protection casket with a forest-green interior, the same model the singer James Brown had been buried in. When she died, it would be slid into a prepaid aboveground vault. Her soaring rhetoric seemed to refer to something far different from the caskets I had seen at Westwind, with crepe pillows and lumpy beds filled with shredded office paper like my cat used in her litter box.

At the end of the casket slideshow, Professor Diaz briefly showed us a picture of the dirtiest, most soot-stained cremation retort I had ever seen. Paola slid over to me and whispered, 'Why does that cremation chamber look like it's from the Holocaust or something?'

'I think it's a veiled warning,' I whispered back.

'Yeah, like, 'So, anyone here want to be cremated instead of buried? Well, come on down, this is where you'll end up. Muahaha.''

★   ★   ★

In the second semester we began embalming lab, the class I feared the most. I had seen embalming in action many a time, but had little interest in performing it myself. Our embalming instructor wore a tie covered in the books of the Bible and would bless us all with the sign of the cross as he dismissed the class. He had faith that, as soon-to-be embalmers, we were doing God's work.

It was evident I had no place in 'traditional' funeral service. I hated embalming lab and the head-to-toe biohazard-resistant protective gear we were forced to wear. The personal protective equipment, or PPEs, were only available in a sickly shade of light blue, making the students look like a cross between the stars of a deadly-disease-outbreak film and overweight Smurfs. More than the outfits (admittedly a frivolous concern), I also hated that our lab bodies were the indigent and homeless dead of Los Angeles County.

The county of Los Angeles has, depending on the year, more than 80,000 homeless men and women living within its borders. More citizens live on the streets in L.A. than in New York, Chicago, and San Francisco *combined*. A mere ten minutes away from the latest big-budget film premiere is a section of downtown known as Skid Row, a pop-up tent city of homeless men and women, many of them mentally disturbed and dependent on drugs. In L.A., the gap between the haves and the have-nots is more like a chasm.

When a celebrity dies in Los Angeles, the news is greeted with tremendous fuss. Michael Jackson's body warranted a private helicopter escort to the L.A. County Coroner's and hundreds of thousands of mourners observed his funeral in person and on the Internet. His body, like those of the medieval saints, was a relic, an object of public adoration.

Not so the bodies of the homeless. They are a rotting burden that must be disposed of on the government's dime. I know these bodies well. They were embalming practice.

Every week a volunteer from Cypress College went to retrieve bodies from the L.A. County Morgue. We fetched our victims from a special fridge (really a vault) full of the unclaimed. The morgue attendant opened the refrigeration unit to reveal *hundreds* of identical white body bags, stacked five shelves high. They are what mortician Thomas Lynch calls 'larger than life-size sperm' for the way hospitals and coroners' offices tie the bags tight around the deceased's feet. It is an entire city of dead bodies, a frozen sperm necropolis.

This fridge is where the dead wait. Weeks pass into months as the county tries to find someone to claim the body. When the trail ends, a county-provided cremation will take place. Starting early in the morning, while some young starlet stumbles drunkenly out of a Hollywood club, bodies are already burning. Having been reduced to ash, they are placed in a container, labelled, and put on a shelf. That shelf is a burgeoning necropolis of its own, and the remains will wait there even longer. They'll wait until the bureaucratic channels have run dry, and the government is finally satisfied that nobody is coming to retrieve the anonymous tin of ashes.

In bad economies, major cities see a drastic increase in unclaimed bodies, not all of them homeless, or even without a family. A son may have loved his mother, but if his house is in foreclosure and his car repossessed, his mother's body might shift from relic to burden very quickly.

Evergreen Cemetery is the oldest cemetery in Los Angeles, established in 1877. Buried on its grounds are former Los Angeles mayors and congressmen and even film stars. Once a year, in a small section where the grass is brown and the markers almost unnoticeable, L.A. County workers dig a large hole. Into the hole they will dump, one after another, almost two thousand sets of unclaimed cremated remains, a thick, grey cloud of dust rising above the digger. They replace a thin layer of topsoil and mark the area with a plaque stating the year they were put in the ground.

Some bodies are 'lucky' enough to visit Cypress College before this anonymous ceremony, where they are laid out on embalming tables and surrounded on all sides by the student Smurf brigade in our protective outfits. We spent the first semester of embalming lab learning where the arteries and veins were, often through trial and error. Someone would slice open the upper thigh in the incorrect place, only to say, 'D'oh! The femoral artery is actually down here.' If at first you don't succeed, slice, slice again.

Outside the embalming laboratory was a stack of trade magazines from the Dodge Company (no relation to the automobiles), which sells embalming and restorative chemicals. Their trade magazine is full of tips 'n' tricks to use with their products.

'Fills! Plumps! Firms!'

'Dryene! Stay Cream! Looks like a dream!'

There were products for sealing skin, hydrating skin, dehydrating skin, firming skin, and bleaching skin. Products to prevent the body from leaking, smelling, and turning strange shades of orange (mental note). Products for curling hair and blushing cheeks and moisturising lips.

My personal favourite was Tim Collison's article 'Cosmetic Considerations for the Infant Death,' a fancy way of saying 'Make-up for Dead Babies.' The three pictures accompanying the article were of a darling living baby, Mr. Collison himself, and a well-lit shot of Dodge's patented Airbrush Cosmetics Deluxe Kit, presumably perfect for use with infants.

If you are like me, your first response might be, 'Gosh, I don't think dead babies really need make-up.' Mr. Collison disagrees with you. He wants to ensure that funeral professionals place 'the tiny body in the casket to look as natural as possible.'

Mortuary schools no longer teach students that they are embalming to make the dead bodies look 'lifelike.' 'Lifelike' makes people think the dead might actually come back to life. The word of choice in the industry is now 'natural.' Embalmers 'restore the body to a natural appearance.'

According to Mr. Collison, the first step to applying 'natural' baby make-up is to preserve the heck out of the baby in question: 'The use of a cosmetic arterial chemical with a humectant base such as Plasdopake or Chromatech, along with sufficient amounts of accessory chemicals, will supply the needed preservation.'

Plasdopake or Chromatech might provide an excellent base for cosmetics, but the downy hair on a newborn's face can be such an impediment. Best to go ahead and shave the baby. Be careful, though, 'the shaving of an infant requires extra care.'

Finally, be aware that a baby's facial pores are much smaller than their adult counterparts. You might think you can use the same old oil- or paraffin-based cream cosmetics you use on adults, but nay. They would make the baby look waxy and not 'produce a natural appearance.' There's that *natural* again.

Often our assigned research papers required us to consult and interview 'funeral industry professionals.' Mike and Bruce served as my funeral professionals. Phone calls with them made me think that perhaps I had left Westwind too soon. After a year there I was still learning so much; it was imprudent for me to waltz out.

Most of all I missed their straight talk.

When I asked Bruce about whether a corpse is going to 'go bad' if not embalmed right away, he laughed derisively, even though he was a long-time embalmer and educator himself. 'The whole 'body going bad' thing has really got blown out of proportion. Granted, if you're in a hundred and ten degrees with no air conditioning, like, the middle of the Amazon rain forest, you gonna want to take care of that. Otherwise, that body isn't going to go rotten in the next hour. It's crazy how funeral homes really think that.'

Mortuary school made me tense to the point of physical illness. The longer you spend doing something you don't believe in, the more the systems of your body rebel. The months drifted by and I was plagued by sore throats, muscle spasms, mouth ulcers. As Dr. Frankenstein ruminated while working to create his monster, 'My heart often sickened at the work of my hands.' It was a stressful environment and a financially foolish decision on my part. But I would have forked out my life savings to anyone who could have let me skip embalming lab and not fail the class.

Granted, I was far from the only student made tense by mortuary school. There was a woman in the programme who would stand outside the building chain-smoking, her hands trembling. She often broke down crying during exams and twice, notably, during labs: once while viciously jamming a metal suction tube into a dead man's foot and once while applying practice curls to a plastic head. I had named my plastic head Maude. My classmate was *not* on a first-name basis with hers.

More and more I began to cherish the idea of the home funeral. I had never forgotten about my original dream of owning a funeral home. The dream of La Belle Mort had morphed into the dream of Undertaking L.A. At Undertaking L.A., families could reclaim the process of dying, washing, dressing, and attending to the body as humans had done for thousands of years. Family members would remain with the body, free to mourn and care for their loved one in a supportive, realistic environment. Such an idea was taboo at mortuary school, where wisdom held that embalming kept a corpse 'sanitary.' No wonder Bruce said funeral directors were telling families that dead bodies were a threat to public health: *they were learning that dead bodies were a threat to public health.*

★ ★ ★

I inched toward graduation and passed the exams to become a licensed funeral director

272

in the state of California. My reveries of galloping into the sunset to start Undertaking L.A. were dampened by financial realities. I had put myself in debt to go to Deth Skool and thus lacked the capital, and perhaps the experience, to open my own funeral home. I had to get another job in the death industry.

One option was moving to Japan, where they were desperate to hire trained embalmers from the United States and Canada. Embalming is a recent development in Japan, where they call it 'death medicine.' One Canadian embalmer who moved to Japan to work described placing bandages on the embalmed corpse to make it look like a medical procedure. Appealing as it would have been to live overseas, I wasn't about to act as the colonialist bearer of ill-advised deathways.

Professor Diaz told me that it would be hard to get hired at a crematorium in Southern California. For that type of physical work, 'they can just get an immigrant to do it.' Though insensitive, she was being honest; this was what crematorium owners had told her.

On the opposite end of the death spectrum was someplace like Forest Lawn Memorial Park, Jessica Mitford's arch-nemesis, the 'Disneyland of Death.' Forest Lawn had expanded to multiple locations across Southern California. Everyone knew Forest Lawn. Their billboards soar high over Los Angeles, picturing a forty-foot-tall elderly couple dressed in white linen. Their heads thrown back in laughter, the couple holds hands and walks along the beach at sunset. They're revelling in their golden years, beaming at each other, just here to gently remind you (in tiny print at the bottom of the billboard) that there is a memorial park available should you wish to prepay for your funeral.

A group of Forest Lawn representatives filled the lobby of Cypress College. It was billed as a job fair, although the 'fair' element fell somewhat flat, as only Forest Lawn was represented. One of the representatives gave a talk to our graduating class.

'Our founder, Hubert Eaton, was a revolutionary!' she gushed. 'Surely you've learned about the wonderful things he has done for the death industry. And it's a wonderful place to work. Such good benefits — people retire from our company.'

At Cypress, the all-female representative army looked just like Evelyn Waugh had described, 'that new race of exquisite, amiable, efficient young ladies' whom he had met everywhere in the United States. They wore matching grey suits and blank stares reminiscent of the Manson family. The Eaton family, if you will, here to gain recruits for the beautiful death brigade.

I filled out their massive employment application and forced myself to turn it in. I had to wait my turn while they interviewed several male students in the mortuary programme, for whom they made no effort to hide their preference.

'Well, I am looking for a job as an arrangement counselor. I do have experience in that area,' I began.

'Now, we call those 'memorial counsellors,' and we don't have anything like that available,' the representative cooed. 'You don't want to be an embalmer?'

'Um, no.'

'Well, perhaps you would be interested in our student programme, where we allow selected students to work part-time at services, giving directions to the families, et cetera. Oh! But look, it says here you are graduating this year, you wouldn't want that.'

'Oh, well, sure I would. I really want to work for your company!' I said with as much vigour as possible, forcing the bile down the back of my throat. I felt gross the rest of the day.

Over the next month I applied everywhere, knowing where I actually wanted to be was back in the trenches, with dead bodies, with real grief and real death. I heard back from two places: a very fancy mortuary/cemetery combination, and a crematorium. I decided to show up at both interviews looking well put together and let fate decide.

Body Van

The cemetery was Old Hollywood glamorous. It wasn't Forest Lawn, but it was close. Turning off the road through the decorative gates was like entering Mount Olympus. A white-columned mansion sat high atop a hill, with a twelve-tiered water fountain cascading below it. It was a wonderland, where a single burial plot could cost tens of thousands of dollars.

I was meeting with the general manager to interview for a job as a funeral director. After a few minutes he came sweeping into the lobby with a plate of chocolate-chip cookies. Directing me into an elevator, he said, 'Here, cookies. Take one.' It felt rude to say no. Afraid to interview with chocolate on my teeth, I gracelessly held the sweet burden in my hand through the entire interview.

We got off the elevator and he led me into his office, which had floor-to-ceiling windows looking out over his death utopia. He delivered a thirty-minute monologue on the pros and cons of his establishment. I would be hired to make funeral arrangements, but, he warned, 'Don't be surprised if the family treats you like a butler — that's the kind of people they are. Here, well, you're the help.'

I would handle the arrangements for everyone *except* the celebrities. He did all the celebrity calls. 'Look,' he said by way of explanation, 'last month when [redacted] died, his service time leaked to the media. Of course, all the paparazzi were swarming the gates. I need that kind of publicity like I need a *fist in my ass*, if you get me. I handle the celebrities now.'

This wasn't my ideal employment situation, but at least the cemetery wasn't run by one of the big funeral corporations. Even better, he swore up and down that I wouldn't have to upsell anything to families: more expensive caskets, extended services, fancy golden urns. No lines like 'Are you sure Mom wouldn't have wanted the rosewood casket? Didn't she deserve a dignified send-off?' were required to earn my bonus. It seemed like a good enough place to recover for a while, licking my wounds from mortuary school.

After telling me I was hired, making me fill out my tax form, and showing me my new office, I didn't hear from him for a month. I had erroneously thought that his 'fist in my ass' speech meant I was part of the team. Apparently there are far more intimate rungs on the funeral-service ladder, because I eventually got a curt e-mail from his secretary informing me they had decided to 'hire internally' instead.

My second interview was at a crematorium, a Westwind of magnificent proportions, a veritable disposal factory. It cremated thousands of bodies a year in a sizeable warehouse in Orange County. It was run by Cliff, a man who spoke in the same flat monotone as Mike, leading me to believe the speech pattern is a job requirement. He also took the place very seriously, having built the business to a size sufficient to support his real passion, competition-level Spanish Andalusian horses. I got the job.

My position would not be a crematorium operator, but a body-transport driver. Most crematoriums receive bodies in deliveries of one to four at a time, depending on their source of origin. My body van, a big diesel-fuel Dodge Sprinter with built-in shelves, held eleven dead bodies at once. Twelve at a pinch, with one corpse tilted at a slight angle.

With my eleven corpses in tow I drove hither and thither across Southern California — San Diego, Palm Springs, Santa Barbara — to retrieve the dead and bring them back to the crematorium. Hauling, lifting, and driving filled my daily schedule.

In my new job I was no longer the belle of my own little ball as I had been at Westwind. I was a mere piece of a puzzle, a specialised labourer. My position was a product of Jessica Mitford's influence, the result of her direct-cremation vision achieving ubiquity, on its way to supreme popularity. California was once again the leader in this new way of death, as it had been with Forest Lawn, as it had been with Mitford, as it had been with Bayside Cremation.

The crematorium was manned by three young Latino men from East Los Angeles, working in shifts all hours of the day and night (and on weekends) to perform cremations in the colossal machines whose fires constantly burned. There was the good — the very sweet Manuel, who always helped me unload my bodies from the van at the end of the day; the bad — the tattooed Emiliano, who made sure to tell me he was looking to get a white girl pregnant; and the ugly — Ricky, who cornered and threatened me in one of the cooling fridges for stacking the bodies in a manner not to his liking.

There was a never-ending stream of decedents who required fetching. On Christmas Eve I got a call from the woman who ran the facility in San Diego: 'Caitlin, there are too many bodies here, we need you tonight.'

So in the middle of the night, while others snuggled in their beds, dreaming sugarplum dreams, my van zoomed from Los Angeles to San Diego and back like a depressing Santa Claus with even more depressing cargo. 'The bodies were stacked in the reefer with care, with hope that the body van soon would be there . . . '

If there was one luxury I had as captain of the Good Ship Body Van, it was time to think. Driving more than 350 miles a day as a long-haul corpse trucker gives one ample time to ponder. Some days I listened to books on tape (*Moby-Dick* on eighteen unabridged CDs, thank you very much). Other days it was the Christian talk radio that starts to come in clearly as soon as you leave metropolitan Los Angeles. But mostly I thought about death.

Every culture has death values. These values are transmitted in the form of stories and myths, told to children starting before they are old enough to form memories. The beliefs children grow up with give them a framework to make sense of and take control of their lives. This need for meaning is why some believe in an intricate system of potential afterlives, others believe sacrificing a certain animal on a certain day leads to healthy crops, and still others believe the world will end when a ship constructed with the untrimmed nails of the dead arrives carrying a corpse army to do battle with the gods at the end of days. (Norse mythology will always be the most metal, sorry.)

But there is something deeply unsettling — or deeply thrilling, depending on how you view it — about what is happening to our death values. There has *never* been a time in the history of the world when a culture has broken so completely with traditional methods of body disposition and beliefs surrounding mortality. There have been times when humans were driven to break tradition by necessity — for example, deaths on a foreign battle-field. But for the most part, when a person dies, they are disposed of like their mother and father were, and like *their* mothers and fathers were. Hindus were cremated, elite Egyptians entombed with their organs in jars, Viking warriors buried in ships. And now, the cultural norm is that Americans are either embalmed and buried, or cremated. But culture no longer dictates that we *must* do those things, out of belief or obligation.

Historically, death rituals have, without question, been tied to religious beliefs. But our world is becoming increasingly secular. The fastest-growing religion in America is 'no religion' — a group that comprises almost 20 per cent of the population in the United States. Even those who identify as having strong religious beliefs often feel their once-strong death rituals have been commoditised and hold less meaning for them. At a time like this, there is no limit to our creativity in creating rituals relevant to our modern lives. The freedom is exciting, but it is also a burden. We cannot possibly live without a relationship to our mortality, and developing secular methods for addressing death will become more critical as each year passes.

I started to put essays and manifestos on the Internet under the name 'The Order of the Good Death,' looking for people who shared my desire for change. One such person was Jae Rhim Lee, an MIT-trained designer and artist who created a full-body suit for a human to wear for burial. The 'Infinity Burial Suit,' which might be described as ninja couture, features a dendritic pattern of white thread spreading out across the black fabric. Lee crafted the thread from mushroom spores, which she specially engineered to consume parts of the human body using her own skin, hair, and nails. This may sound like a *Soylent Green* future, but Lee is actually training the mushrooms to remove toxins from our bodies as they decompose the human corpse.

After seeing a demonstration of her work at the MAK Center for Art and Architecture in Los Angeles, we met at a taco van and talked for hours on a bus-stop bench on Olympic and La Brea. I was grateful to talk to someone interested in pushing the boundaries of body disposal; she was grateful that someone in the traditional funeral industry was willing to listen to her ideas. We both agreed that inspiring people to engage with the reality of their inevitable decomposition was a noble purpose. She gave me a bucket of the flesh-eating mushroom prototype, which I attempted (and failed) to keep alive in my garage. Not feeding it enough flesh, I reckon.

For years, while working at Westwind and attending mortuary school, I had been afraid to discuss cultural death denial in public. The Internet is not always the kindest of forums, especially for young women. Tucked away in the comment section of my kitschy web series 'Ask a Mortician,' there are enough misogynistic comments to last a lifetime. Yes, gentlemen, I'm aware I give your penis rigor mortis. It wasn't just the anonymous basement dwellers who took issue with me. People in the funeral industry weren't always thrilled that I was sharing what they perceived to be privileged 'behind the black curtain' knowledge. 'I'm sure she's just having some fun. But since fun has no place in the funeral industry, I wouldn't go to her for my loved one.' To this day the National Funeral Directors Association, the industry's largest professional association, won't comment on me.

But as I grew bolder, people came out of the woodwork. Crawled out of the coffin, if you will. People from all different disciplines — funeral directors, hospice workers, academics, filmmakers, artists — had wanted to discover how death works in our lives.

I wrote a lot of letters, sometimes out of the blue. One such recipient was Dr. John Troyer, a professor at the University of Bath's Centre for Death and Society. Dr. Troyer, whose PhD dissertation was titled 'Technologies of the Human Corpse,' is studying crematoriums that capture the excess heat from the cremation process and put it to use elsewhere — heating other buildings, or even, as one crematorium in Worcestershire did, a local swimming pool, saving taxpayers £14,500 a year. It is a way to make the cremation process, which uses as much energy as a 500-mile car trip for a single body, more energy efficient. Luckily Dr. Troyer was willing to talk with me, even with my crude e-mail subject line, 'Fan Gurl!'

It was a relief to find others like me; it removed the stigma and alienation. These were practitioners shifting our relationship with death, pulling the shroud off our death-ways and getting to the hard work of facing the inevitable.

This work drove me internally. Externally, I was just the body-van driver. Three times a week I would drive my eleven corpses up the I–5 from San Diego and pass through the immigration checkpoint. My large, unmarked white van moved slowly towards the front of the inspection line, looking far more suspicious than the Priuses and Volvos in the other lanes. I would find myself hoping to be stopped, if only as a break from the monotony. In my mind, this is how the scene would go:

'You don't got any *inmigrantes* back there, do ya, missy?'

'No *inmigrantes*, Officer. Just eleven people,' I'd reply, and, whipping off my sunglasses, 'former US citizens.'

'Former?'

'Oh, they're dead, Officer. Real dead.'

Unfortunately, every time the van rolled up and the officer saw a young white woman at the wheel, he or she would wave us right on through. I could have smuggled hundreds of Mexicans into the country in cardboard cremation containers. I could have been a drug mule. I could be a rich woman by now.

With as much time as I was spending on

the road, my main fear was getting into an accident, crashing on the freeway. I imagined the back doors of my van flying open, all eleven passengers being hurled out. The police show up amid chaos and confusion. Eleven fatalities — but why are these people so cold, with no signs of bodily trauma?

Once the smoke cleared and they discovered that all these fatalities were pre-dead, I'd become an Internet meme, my little head grimacing in a Photoshopped *Wizard of Oz*-style corpse tornado.

But every day I made it back to the crematorium with my eleven bodies. When I pulled up behind the warehouse, Emiliano would be playing his accordion in the parking lot along with the Norteño music blasting from the stereo in his Cadillac. The soundtrack to my body unloading.

But the day I almost died, I wasn't in the body van. I was driving my ancient Volkswagen through Salton Sea, California. Salton Sea is a man-made saltwater lake smack dab in the middle of the Southern California desert. One idea in the 1960s had been to redesign it as a resort destination, an alternative to Palm Springs. Now, instead of martinis, Hawaiian shirts, and water-skiing, abandoned mobile homes line a morass of brown water with an unbelievable stench. Massive fish die-offs have littered the shoreline with fish and pelican corpses. The satisfying crunch of the sand beneath your feet comes courtesy of thousands of dried bones. I had made the four-hour pilgrimage from Los Angeles to visit this monument to decay. Some consider it gauche to visit so-called ruin porn, but I like to witness first-hand the way nature will declare war against our hubris, building in places unintended for human habitation.

As I drove towards the northern shore of the thirty-five-mile-long Salton Sea, I chanced upon a dead coyote by the side of the road. This wasn't one of the petite, doglike coyotes sometimes found in urban Los Angeles — it was a beast with a blackened tongue and distended stomach. I made a U-turn and returned to inspect him, undaunted by the suspicious locals in their vans and ATVs.

Perhaps this coyote was an omen. The coyote and/or the fish graveyard at the Salton Sea. And/or the old women riding golf carts in pink Juicy Couture tracksuits. They all might have been omens.

Darkness had fallen before I departed for Los Angeles. The four westbound lanes of the I–10 freeway passed through Palm Springs, filled with Sunday revellers heading home. I was driving my Volkswagen in the outside lane at a steady 75 miles per hour. The back left side of the car began to shake, and I felt the dull thud of a tyre blowout. I put on my blinker to move into the middle lane, miffed at my bad luck.

But it turned out a flat tyre wasn't the problem. The bearings had slipped loose and the entire wheel had begun spinning off the axle. Finally, bolts snapped and off it came, leaving a gaping hole where the wheel once was.

With only three wheels, the car spun wildly out of control. I spiralled across four lanes, raising a rooster tail of sparks as bare metal scraped against asphalt. Time seemed to slow as the Volkswagen performed its deadly dance across the highway. There was a complete, throbbing silence inside the car. The lights from oncoming traffic whirled in a blur around me, the vehicles missing me as if blocked by some miraculous buffer.

More than the loss of control, more than the crushing loneliness of contemporary life, *this* was my worst fear, what Buddhists and medieval Christians referred to as 'the bad death' — a death for which there is no preparation. In the modern era it takes the form of bodies ripped apart in a searing crunch of metal. Never to tell their loved ones how passionately they are loved. Affairs out of order. Funeral desires unknown.

Yet, as I spun and my hands pulled the wheel in some attempt at control, my mind was miles away. At first, a voice said, *Ah, here we go,* and a gentle peace descended. The 'Moonlight Sonata' played and slow motion began. I had no fear. I realised as the car spun that this would not have been a bad death. My four years working with bodies and the families attached to them had made this moment a transcendent experience. My body went limp, waiting to accept the violent impact. It never came.

I slammed into a dirt hill bordering the shoulder of the highway. Facing oncoming traffic head-on, upright, and alive, cars and trucks whizzed by me at dizzying speed, any (or many) of which could have hit me during my swirling journey across the highway. But they hadn't.

Once I had been terrified at the thought of my body being fragmented. No longer. My fear of fragmentation was born from fearing the loss of control. Here was the ultimate loss of control, flung across the freeway, but in the moment there was only calm.

The Art of Dying

There is a mid-fifteenth-century German wood-cut entitled *Triumph over Temptation* that depicts a man lying on his deathbed. The denizens of heaven and hell surround him, fighting over his mortal soul. Demons with twisted porcine faces, claws, and hooves reach towards the bed to drag him down to the fiery underworld; above him, a horde of angels and a floating crucified Jesus pull a tiny version of the man (presumably his soul) upward to heaven. In the midst of all this commotion, the dying man looks positively blissed out, filled with inner Zen. The little smirk on his face tells the viewer what he is thinking: 'Ah yes, death. I've got this.'

The question is: how do we get to be *that* guy? The one who is facing his own death with complete calm, ready to get on with the moving on.

The woodcut represents a popular genre in the late Middle Ages: the Ars Moriendi, or the Art of Dying. Ars Moriendi were instruction manuals that taught Christians how to die the good death, repenting mortal sins and allowing the soul to ascend to heaven. This view of death as an 'art' or 'practice,' rather than an emotionless biological process, can be tremendously empowering.

There is no Art of Dying manual available in our society, so I decided to write my own. It is intended not only for the religious, but also for the growing number of atheists, agnostics, and vaguely 'spiritual' among us. For me, the good death includes being prepared to die, with my affairs in order, the good and bad messages delivered that need delivering. The good death means dying while I still have my mind sharp and aware; it also means dying without having to endure large amounts of suffering and pain. The good death means accepting death as inevitable, and not fighting it when the time comes. This is *my* good death, but as legendary psychotherapist Carl Jung said, 'It won't help to hear what I think about death.' Your relationship to mortality is your own.

I recently sat next to a middle-aged Japanese man on a flight from L.A. to Reno. He was reading a professional magazine called *Topics in Hemorrhoids*, complete with a large-scale photographic cross-section of the anal canal on the cover. Magazines for gastroenterologists do not mess around with metaphorical cover images of sunsets or mountainscapes. I, on the other hand, was reading a professional magazine that proclaimed 'Decay Issue!' on the cover. We looked at each other and smiled, sharing a tacit understanding that our respective publications weren't for popular consumption.

He introduced himself as a doctor and medical-school professor, and I introduced myself as a mortician trying to engage the wider public in a conversation about death. When he found out what I was working on, he said, 'Well, good, I'm glad you're talking about this. By 2020 there will be a huge shortage of physicians and caretakers, but no one wants to talk about it.'

We know that *media vita in morte sumus* or, 'in the midst of life we are in death.' We begin dying the day we are born, after all. But because of advances in medical science, the majority of us will spend the later years of our lives actively dying. The fastest growing segment of the population is over eighty-five, what I would call the aggressively elderly. If you reach eighty-five, not only is there a strong chance you are living with some form of dementia or terminal disease, but statistics show that you have a 50–50 chance of ending up in a nursing home, raising the question of whether a good life is measured in quality or quantity. This slow decline differs sharply from times past, when people tended to die quickly, often in a single day. Post-mortem daguerreotypes from the 1800s picture fresh, young, almost lifelike corpses, many of them victims of scarlet fever or diphtheria. In 1899, a mere 4 per cent of the US population was over sixty-five — forget making it to eighty-five. Now, many will know that death is coming during months or years of deterioration. Medicine has given us the 'opportunity' — loosely defined — to sit at our own wakes.

But this gradual deterioration comes at a terrible cost. There are many ways for a corpse to be disturbing. Decapitated bodies are fairly gruesome, as are those dredged from the water after several days afloat, their green skin sloughing off in strips. But the decubitus ulcer presents a unique psychological horror. The word 'decubitus' comes from the Latin *decumbere*, to lie down. As a rule, bedridden patients have to be moved every few hours, flipped like pancakes to ensure that the weight of their own bodies doesn't press their bones into the tissue and skin, cutting off blood circulation. Without blood flow, tissue begins to decay. The ulcers occur when a patient is left lying in bed for an extended period, as often happens in understaffed nursing homes.

Without some movement, the patient will literally begin to decompose while he or she is still living, eaten alive by their own necrotic tissue. One particular body that came into the preparation room at Westwind I will remember for the rest of my life. She was a ninety-year-old African American woman, brought in from a poorly equipped nursing home, where the patients who weren't bedridden were kept in cheerless holding pens, staring blankly at the walls. As I turned her over to wash her back, I received the ghastly surprise of a gaping, raw wound the size of a football festering on her lower back. It was akin to the gaping mouth of hell. You can almost gaze through such a wound into our dystopian future.

We do not (and will not) have the resources to properly care for our increasing elderly population, yet we insist on medical intervention to keep them alive. To allow them to die would signal the failure of our supposedly infallible modern medical system.

The surgeon Atul Gawande wrote in a devastating New Yorker article on aging that 'there have been dozens of best-selling books on aging but they tend to have titles like 'Younger Next Year,' 'The Fountain of Age,' 'Ageless,' 'The Sexy Years.' Still, there are costs to averting our eyes from the realities.

For one thing, we put off changes that we need to make as a society . . . In thirty years, there will be as many people over eighty as there are under five.'

Year after year my seatmate, the gastroenterologist and professor, encountered firsthand a new crop of students terrified of their own mortality. Even though the elderly population continues to soar, he has fought for years to implement more classes in geriatrics (the study of diseases and treatment in the elderly), and is repeatedly denied. Medical students just aren't choosing geriatric care; the income is too low, the work too brutal. No surprise, medical schools turn out plastic surgeons and radiologists by the boatload.

Gawande, again: 'I asked Chad Boult, the geriatrics professor now at Johns Hopkins, what can be done to ensure that there are enough geriatricians for our country's surging elderly population. 'Nothing,' he said. 'It's too late.''

I was impressed that my doctor-seatmate (and bit of a kindred spirit, really) took such an open approach. He said, 'I tell dying patients that I can prolong their lives, but I can't always cure them. If they choose to prolong, it will mean pain and suffering. I don't ever want to be cruel, but they need to understand the diagnosis.'

'At least your students are learning that from you,' I said, hopeful.

'Well, OK, but here's the thing: my students don't ever want to give a terminal diagnosis. I have to ask, 'Did you fully explain it to them?''

'Even if someone is dying, they just . . . don't tell them?' I asked, shocked.

He nodded. '*They* don't want to face their *own* mortality. They'd rather take an anatomy exam for the eighth time than face a dying person. And the doctors, the old guys, guys my age, they're even worse.'

My grandmother Lucile Caple was eighty-eight when her mind shut down, even though, technically, her body lived on to the age of ninety-two. She had gone to the bathroom in the middle of the night and fallen, hitting her head on the coffee table and developing a subdural haematoma — medical-speak for bleeding around the brain. After a few months in a rehabilitation centre, sharing a room with a woman named Edeltraut Chang (whom I mention only because hers was the greatest name ever assembled), my grandmother came home. But she was never the same, transformed by her brain damage into something of a loony tune — if I may throw around another fancy medical term.

Without medical intervention, Tutu (the Hawaiian word for grandmother) would have died shortly after her traumatic brain injury. But she didn't. Before her mind was blunted, she had insisted, 'For heaven's sake, don't let *me* ever get like that,' yet there she was, stuck in that depressing place between life and death.

After the subdural haematoma, Tutu would tell long, fantastical stories to explain how she had fallen and hurt herself. My favourite was that the city of Honolulu had commissioned her to paint a mural at the entrance to City Hall. While leading her merry team of painters on an artistic quest up a mangrove tree, a branch had broken and she plummeted to the ground below.

One memorable evening Tutu thought my father, whom she had known for forty years, was a maintenance man attempting to make off with her jewellery. My grandfather, who had died several years earlier of Alzheimer's, would pay her post-mortem visits to share classified information from the beyond. According to Tutu, the government had assassinated Grandpa Dayton to cover up the fact that he alone knew the structural reason the levees had failed after Hurricane Katrina.

Tutu was what you'd call a 'tough old broad.' She drank martinis and smoked until the day she died, yet her lungs remained as pink as a baby's bottom (results not typical). She grew up in the Midwest during the Depression, forced to wear the same skirt and blouse every day for an entire year. After she married my grandfather, they lived all over the world, from Japan to Iran, settling in Hawai'i in the 1970s. Their house was one block away from mine.

After the accident, Tutu spent her remaining years living like the Queen of Sheba in her retirement condominium downtown. She had 24/7 care from a Samoan woman named Valerie, who bordered on sainthood. Even towards the end of Tutu's life, as my grandmother slipped further and further into the fog, Valerie would get Tutu out of bed every morning, bathe her, dress her (never forgetting the pearl necklace), and take her on outings about town. When Tutu wasn't well enough to leave the house, Valerie lovingly propped her up with her cigarettes and left CNN on the television set.

The unfortunate truth, and one of the reasons why openly acknowledging death is so crucial, is that most people who linger into extreme old age are nowhere near as lucky as Tutu, with her good retirement plan, devoted caretaker, and Tempur-Pedic adjustable memory-foam bed. Tutu is the exception that proves the tragic rule. Because this ever-growing geriatric army reminds us of our own mortality, we push them into the shadows. Most elderly women (our gender represents the distinct majority of elderfolk) end up in overcrowded nursing homes, waiting in agonising stasis.

By not talking about death with our loved ones, not being clear through advanced directives, DNR (do not resuscitate) orders, and funeral plans, we are directly contributing to this future ... and a rather bleak present, at that. Rather than engage in larger societal discussions about dignified ways for the terminally ill to end their lives, we accept intolerable cases like that of Angelita, a widow in Oakland who covered her head with a plastic bag because the arthritic pain of her gnarled joints was too much to bear. Or that of Victor in Los Angeles, who hanged himself from the rafters of his apartment after his third unsuccessful round of chemotherapy, leaving his son to discover his body. Or the countless bodies with decubitus ulcers, more painful for me to care for than even babies or suicides. When these bodies come into the funeral home, I can only offer my sympathy to their living relatives, and promise to work to ensure that more people are not robbed of a dignified death by a culture of silence.

Even with the knowledge that they may die

a slow, gruelling death, many people still wish to remain kept alive at all costs. Larry Ellison, the third wealthiest man in America, has sunk millions of dollars into research aimed at extending life, because, he says, 'Death makes me very angry. It doesn't make sense to me.' Ellison has made death his enemy and believes that we should expand our arsenal of medical technology to end it altogether.

It is no surprise that the people trying so frantically to extend our lifespans are almost entirely rich, white men. Men who have lived lives of systematic privilege, and believe that privilege should extend indefinitely. I even went on a date with one of them, a PhD candidate in computational biology at the University of Southern California. Isaac started his graduate career in physics, but made the switch once he discovered that, biologically, man does not *have* to age. Perhaps 'discovered' is too strong a word. 'I had the idea that, using the principles of physics and biology, we can engineer and maintain a state of indefinite youth. But when I realised that there were other people already working on it, I was almost like, fuck it,' Isaac explained to me over our organic chicken sandwiches, revealing not a trace of irony.

Though he had seriously pursued rock stardom and considered writing a great novel,

Isaac now waxed poetic on mitochondria and cell death, and the idea of slowing the aging process to a snail's pace. But I was ready for him. 'There is already overpopulation,' I said. 'So much poverty and destruction, we don't have the resources to take care of the people we already have on Earth, forget everyone living forever! And there will still be death by accident. It will just be even more tragic for someone who is supposed to live until three hundred to die at twenty-two.'

Isaac was entirely unmoved. 'This isn't for other people,' he explained. 'This is for me. I'm terrified at the thought of my body decaying. I don't want to die. I want to live forever.'

Death might appear to destroy the meaning in our lives, but in fact it is the very source of our creativity. As Kafka said, 'The meaning of life is that it ends.' Death is the engine that keeps us running, giving us the motivation to achieve, learn, love, and create. Philosophers have proclaimed this for thousands of years just as vehemently as we insist upon ignoring it generation after generation. Isaac was getting his PhD, exploring the boundaries of science, making music *because* of the inspiration death provided. If he lived forever, chances are he would be rendered boring, listless, and unmotivated, robbed of life's richness by dull routine. The great achievements of humanity were born out of the deadlines imposed by death. He didn't seem to realise the fire beneath his ass *was* mortality — the very thing he was attempting to defeat.

★ ★ ★

The morning I got the call about Tutu's death, I was in L.A. at a crematorium, labelling boxes of ashes. After almost a year driving the body van, I had recently moved to a job at a mortuary, running their local office. I was now working with families and coordinating funerals and cremations with doctors, the coroner's office, the county death-certificate office.

The phone rang, with my mother's voice on the other end: 'Valerie just called. She's hysterical. She said Tutu's not breathing. I think she's dead. I used to know what to do, but now I don't. I don't know what to do.'

The remainder of my morning was spent on the phone with family members and the funeral home. It was exactly the same thing I did at work every day, except this was my grandmother, the woman who had lived a block away when I was growing up, who had put me through college and mortuary school, and who called me Caiti-pie.

While they waited for the morticians to arrive, Valerie laid Tutu's corpse out on her bed and dressed her body in a green cashmere sweater and a colourful scarf. My mother texted me a picture. 'Here's Tutu,' it read. Even through the phone, I could tell Tutu looked more peaceful than she had in years. Her face was no longer screwed up in confusion, struggling to understand the rules of the world around her. Tutu's mouth hung open and her face blanched white, but she was a beautiful shell. A relic of the woman she once was. I still treasure this picture.

On my flight to Hawai'i that afternoon I had one of those somnial visions that live between dream and nightmare. I was at the funeral home to see Tutu, and I was led into a room where her emaciated body lay in a glass coffin. Her face was decomposed, bloated and black. She had been embalmed, but something had gone horribly wrong. 'Is she to your liking?' the funeral director asked. 'My God, no! She isn't!' I cried, and grabbed a sheet to cover her. I had told them not to embalm her, and they had done it anyway.

In real life, my family had let me handle the funeral arrangements, as I was, technically, the professional. We had decided on a simple viewing for our family and then a witness cremation. When we came into the viewing room I understood what the man from New Zealand (or was it Australia? I'll probably never know) at Westwind had meant by 'Mom looked better before.' Tutu didn't look like the woman in the picture my mother sent me. Her mouth had been pulled into a grimace with wires and superglue. I knew the tricks. She wore bright-red lipstick in a colour she never wore when she was alive. I couldn't believe I had let my own grandmother's body fall victim to the post-mortem tortures I was fighting against. It demonstrated just how strong a hold the mortuary industry has over our way of death.

My family and I stared down at Tutu's body in the coffin. One of my cousins clumsily touched her hand. Valerie, her carer, approached the casket carrying her four-year-old niece, who would often come to visit Tutu. Valerie let her niece kiss Tutu repeatedly, and she herself began to wail, touching Tutu's face and crying, 'Lucy, Lucy, my beautiful lady' in her lilting Samoan accent. To see her touch the corpse so freely made me ashamed that I had been so awkward. Ashamed that I hadn't pushed harder to keep Tutu's body at home, even when the funeral director had told my mother that keeping the body any longer than two hours was against Hawai'i state law (it's not).

It is never too early to start thinking about your own death and the deaths of those you love. I don't mean thinking about death in obsessive loops, fretting that your husband has been crushed in a horrific car accident, or that your plane will catch fire and plummet from the sky. But rational interaction, that ends with you realising that you will survive the worst, whatever the worst may be. Accepting death doesn't mean that you won't be devastated when someone you love dies. It means you will be able to focus on your grief, unburdened by bigger existential questions like 'Why do people die?' and 'Why is this happening to me?' Death isn't happening to you. Death is happening to us all.

A culture that denies death is a barrier to achieving a good death. Overcoming our fears and wild misconceptions about death will be no small task, but we shouldn't forget how quickly other cultural prejudices — racism, sexism, homophobia — have begun to topple in the recent past. It is high time death had its own moment of truth.

Buddhists say that thoughts are like drops of water on the brain; when you reinforce the same thought, it will etch a new stream into your consciousness, like water eroding the side of a mountain. Scientists confirm this bit of folk wisdom: our neurons break connections and form new pathways all the time. Even if you've been programmed to fear death, that particular pathway isn't set in stone. Each of us is responsible for seeking out new knowledge and creating new mental circuits.

I was not doomed forever to be the child tortured by the sight of a girl falling to her death in a Hawaiian shopping mall. Nor was I doomed forever to be the woman in the redwood forest on the brink of taking her own life rather than submitting to a life consumed by death. Through my interactions with art and literature, and, crucially, through my confrontations with my own mortality, I had rewired my brain's circuits into what Joseph Campbell called a 'bolder, cleaner, more spacious, and fully human life.'

The day of Tutu's viewing, the power had gone out in the funeral home's primary chapel. They decided to trouble-shoot by moving another, much larger family into our room. Dozens of people crowded outside, pushing up against the glass, waiting for me and my relatives to finish our viewing. It was clear that we were an inconvenience to this family and to the funeral home employees. I thought, for the three hundredth time that day, how different this would have been if I hadn't caved and we had kept Tutu at home.

When the crowd finally became too cumbersome to ignore, we cut the service short. Our family practically had to jog down the hall to keep up with the funeral director wheeling Tutu's casket to the crematorium. The crematorium operator had rolled her into the flames before my family even had time to gather. I missed Westwind, which, despite its industrial décor, did have a certain openness and warmth, with its vaulted ceilings and skylights (and with Chris to light the candle as the machine door closed). I felt like I had failed my family.

Someday, I would like to open my own crematorium. Not an industrial warehouse, but a space both intimate and open, with floor-to-ceiling windows to let the sunshine in and keep the weirdo death stigma out. Through the reach of the Order of the Good Death, I was able to work with two Italian architects to design such a place, where a family can witness the body loading into the cremation machine with light streaming in through the glass, giving the illusion they are outdoors in a place of serenity and nature, not of industry.

I also want better municipal, state, and federal laws in North America, which would allow not only for more natural burials but also for open-air pyres and grounds where bodies can be laid out in the open and consumed by nature. We don't need to stop at green or natural burial. 'Burial' comes from the Anglo-Saxon word *birgan*, 'to conceal.' Not everyone wants to be concealed under the earth. I don't want to be concealed. Ever since my dark night of the soul in the redwood forest, I've believed the animals I've consumed my whole life should someday have their turn with me. The ancient Ethiopians would place their dead in the lake where they fished, so the fish would have the opportunity to receive back the nutrients. The earth is expertly designed to take back what it has created. Bodies left for carrion in enclosed, regulated spaces could be the answer to the environmental problems of burial and cremation. There is no limit to where our engagement with death can take us.

We can wander further into the death dystopia, denying that we will die and hiding dead bodies from our sight. Making that choice means we will continue to be terrified and ignorant of death, and the huge role it plays in how we live our lives. Let us instead reclaim our mortality, writing our own Ars Moriendi for the modern world with bold, fearless strokes.

Prodigal Daughter
(An Epilogue of Sorts)

Four years after leaving my job at Westwind Cremation & Burial, I stood, once again, outside the front gate. I rang the bell, the prodigal daughter returned home to the corpse-burning hearth. After a few moments, Mike came out to let me in.

'Well, look at who it is,' he said with a smirk. 'You keep coming back like a bad penny. Come inside with me, I'm fingerprinting a body.'

We passed through the lobby and back into the crematorium, and I still felt some of the same reverence I'd had when I first walked into that cavernous room five years earlier. In the middle of the room was a cot holding the body of an elderly woman. She was surrounded by four sheets of white paper, filled along the edges with black thumbprints.

'OK, so you're literally fingerprinting a body,' I said. 'I was wondering if that was a metaphor or something. Is this for one of those Thumbie necklaces?' I asked, recalling the company that laser-etches fingerprints into memorial necklaces. It seemed even Westwind couldn't escape the funeral industry's siren song to personalisation.

'Yeah, you got it,' Mike said as he lifted the woman's hand and gently wiped the black ink off her thumb. He applied a fresh coat and pressed her thumb to paper for the umpteenth time. 'This is the stuff I get obsessed with, man. None of these are right yet. I'm cremating the body today — I have to get a good print.'

Mike went to answer the phone, and I pulled out my notebook. I had come to research this book, to ask questions, to confirm stories. I had even made an official appointment, like a professional. Mike walked back into the room and asked, deadpan, 'So are you around here for the afternoon? We need you to go on a removal out in Piedmont. I have a service today, I can't do it, and Chris needs a second person.'

I had been back for all of five minutes and already I was being sent out on a removal. It was as if I had never left, death's indomitable schedule sending me straight back to work.

'What the hell, yeah, I'll go,' I replied, trying to sound nonchalant at the prospect. To be honest, I was pretty excited to be back on the team.

'Good. Chris is on his way back from the

coroner's now. By the way, I didn't tell him you were coming. It's a surprise.'

When Chris walked through the door, a look of disbelief flickered over his face. The look passed quickly. 'I knew you'd be back, Cat.'

Later, as we drove through the winding hills up to Piedmont, Chris asked where I was staying.

'Oakland, with friends,' I answered.

'That's good, it means you don't have to go to that devil city,' he replied, pointing vaguely in the direction of San Francisco.

'So I hear that you're writing a 'book,'' he continued, making air quotes with his fingers.

'Well, it's a real book, Chris. Not a hypothetical one.'

'Why would you ever write about us? We're dull. You should make it fictionalised characters. Like us, but better.'

'I would argue that you guys are pretty interesting.'

'It's dull as tombs here. It's a good thing you got out while you still could. Shame you didn't leave the industry altogether.'

We pulled up to a large old house with a white picket fence covered in vines.

'Well, this is a nice place. You got lucky, Cat. The body I picked up yesterday was a decomp. It purged all over me. Although that guy was in a pretty nice apartment too. You just never know what's inside,' Chris mused, pulling the gurney out from the back of the van.

We returned to Westwind with the body of Ms. Sherman, a beautiful woman in her mid-eighties with thick white hair. Her body had been washed by her family and covered in fresh flowers. Before sliding her onto the cot I grabbed her hand, colder than a living human's, warmer than a mere inanimate object. My reaction to seeing her laid out this way was a reminder of how much I had changed since I first started at Westwind; whereas before bodies had scared me, now there was nothing more elegant in my eyes than a corpse in its natural state, prepared with dignity by her own family.

After unloading Ms. Sherman, Chris went out again to retrieve the latest batch of babies. Mike was up front making funeral arrangements with a family. With no one to talk to, I decided to put Ms. Sherman away in the refrigeration unit. As I taped and labelled her cremation container, the cardboard edge gave me the same razor-thin paper cut it had a million times in the past. 'Oh, what the — really?' I said to no one in particular.

Westwind's newest crematorium operator, a young woman named Cheryl, came into the crematorium, clearly confused by my presence there. After I explained who I was, she clumsily shook my hand and walked back out. Jerry, the man originally hired to replace me when I left Westwind, had died of fast-moving cancer a few months earlier. He was only forty-five.

As I was leaving for the day, Bruce stopped by to pick up a cheque for several embalmings he had done the week prior. 'Caitlin! How you doing? I've seen those videos you do online. What's your website?'

'The Order of the Good Death.'

'Yeah, yeah, and the videos, the Question for a Mortician ones? Yeah, they're good, they're good.'

'Thanks, Bruce, I'm glad you like them.'

'You know what you need to do? I have a plan for you. You need to do a show at night, like with monster movies and such. A show like Answer a Mortician . . . is that what it's called? Anyway, it would be like that. Paired with like, creature features. There was one on cable access in the '70s. I tried to get my buddy at KTVU to bring it back. Everybody watches these monster movies on a Saturday. Like Svengoolie or who's that woman — Vampira. Cult classic stuff.'

'I think I'd make a pretty poor Vampira substitute.'

'No! Don't worry about it, you've already got the right hair for it,' he assured me. 'I'm gonna talk to my buddy.'

★ ★ ★

On my way out of San Francisco I drove by Rondel Place. My former apartment had been stripped of its dull pink paint and refashioned as an elegant Victorian, right down to the gilded trimmings. I had a feeling my old room no longer rented for $500 a month. A handcrafted bicycle-messenger-bag shop had opened up across the street, and high-tech cameras at the end of the alley threatened to expose potential miscreants. The sidewalks on the surrounding streets had been repaved with glitter. Glitter. It was a shocking change from the Rondel I knew, but as the joke goes: 'Q: What's the definition of a gentrifier? A: Someone who arrived five minutes after you did.'

Halfway to Los Angeles, I stopped for the night at a small boarding house in the seaside town of Cambria. This was one of my favourite places in California, but I was filled with anxiety that I couldn't place.

In 1961, a paper in the *Journal of Abnormal and Social Psychology* laid out the seven reasons humans fear dying:

1. My death would cause grief to my relatives and friends.
2. All my plans and projects would come to an end.
3. The process of dying might be painful.
4. I could no longer have any experiences.
5. I would no longer be able to care for my dependents.
6. I am afraid of what might happen to me if there is a life after death.
7. I am afraid of what might happen to my body after death.

The anxiety I felt was no longer caused by the fear of an afterlife, of pain, of a void of nothingness, or even a fear of my own decomposing corpse. *All my plans and projects would come to an end.* The last thing preventing me from accepting death was, ironically, my desire to help people accept death.

I dined at Cambria's one Thai restaurant and walked back to the boarding house. The streets were quiet and empty. Through the thick fog, I could barely make out a sign above the road: Cemetery, 1 mile. I strode up the hill, walking straight down the centre of the road with big, bold steps — bigger and bolder than my cardiovascular health should have allowed for. The full moon peeked out from the clouds, lighting up the pine trees and causing the fog to glow an eerie white.

The road came to an abrupt end at the Cambria Cemetery, est. 1870. Stepping over the small metal chain, a rather ineffectual deterrent against trespassers, I walked down through the rows of graves. To my left the leaves crunched, breaking the silence. Standing on the path in front of me was an enormous buck, its antlers framed in the mist. We stood looking at each other for several moments.

The comedian Louis C.K. talks about how 'mysterious and beautiful' deer *seem* until you live in the country and deer are shitting in your yard and causing highway accidents. But this night, framed majestically in the fog, you had better believe that damn deer appeared like a spiritual messenger.

The buck slipped past the headstones and back into the trees. I was exhausted. No matter how bold my steps had been in the climb up to the cemetery, it was adrenaline that could not be sustained. I almost fell to the ground, mercifully covered in soft pine needles, and leaned against a tree between Howard J. Flannery (1903–1963) and a grave marked only with a small metal sign reading A SOARING SPIRIT, A PEACEFUL HEART.

I sat next to Howard J. Flannery for so long that the fog lifted. The full moon stood out crisp and white and thousands of stars appeared against the black sky.

It was complete, silver silence. Not a cricket, not a breath of wind, just the moon and the old headstones. I thought of the things that culture teaches us to fear about being in a cemetery at night. A floating spectre appearing, its demon red eyes aglow. A zombie pushing its bloated, decaying hand out of a nearby grave. Organ music swelling, owls hooting, gates creaking. They seemed like cheap gimmicks; any one of them would have shattered the stillness and perfection of death. Maybe we create the gimmicks precisely for that reason, because the stillness itself is too difficult to contemplate.

At the moment I was alive with blood coursing through my veins, floating above the putrefaction below, many potential tomorrows on my mind. Yes, my projects could lie fragmented and unfinished after my death. Unable to choose how I would die physically, I could only choose how I would die mentally. Whether my mortality caught me at twenty-eight or ninety-three, I made the choice to die content, slipped into the nothingness, my atoms becoming the very fog that cloaked the trees. The silence of death, of the cemetery, was no punishment, but a reward for a life well lived.

Acknowledgements

It takes a village to raise a death book. Is this a thing people say? It should be. If you'll indulge me, there are people to whom tremendous credit is due.

The wonderful team at W. W. Norton, so good at their jobs it makes me uncomfortable. Ryan Harrington, Steve Colca, Erin Sinesky-Lovett, Elisabeth Kerr, and countless others.

Special thanks to Tom Mayer, my editor, who never coddled me and took stern issue with my adverbs. Bless you and your children's children, Tom Mayer.

The Ross Yoon Agency, especially Anna Sproul-Latimer, who did coddle me, holding my hand like a wee babe in the woods through all parts of this process.

My parents John and Stephanie Doughty, upstanding folk who love and support their daughter even when she's chosen a life-in-death. Mom, I'm probably not going to win that Oscar . . . so this is it.

I'm loth to think of the poor-sad-no-good-pathetic thing I would be without David Forrest and Mara Zehler.

I realise this book makes it seem like I have

no friends. I do, uh . . . promise. They are brilliant, thoughtful people all over the world who went, 'You're going to be a mortician? Yeah, that makes sense.'

Some of those friends were the keen eyes that read and reread this bloated beast through years of drafts: Will C White, Will Slocombe, Sarah Fornace, Alex Frankel, and Usha Herold Jenkins.

Bianca Daalder-van Iersel and Jillien Kahn, both of whom did great things to keep my brain intact and functioning. Paola Caceres, who provided the same service in mortuary school.

Lawyer-extraordinaire Evan Hess, for keeping me out of real bad things.

The members of the Order of the Good Death and the alternative death community at large, who inspire me daily to do better work.

Dodai Stewart at Jezebel, a big reason people care.

Finally, the men who ushered me into the death industry and taught me how to be an ethical, hard-working funeral director: Michael Tom, Chris Reynolds, Bruce Williams, and Jason Bruce. To be honest, it wasn't until I was out in the cold, harsh death world that I realised just how good I had it at the safe, professional, and well-run funeral home I've called Westwind.

Notes on Sources

The Caribbean American writer Audre Lorde wrote, 'There are no new ideas. There are only new ways of making them felt.' Writing this book was a six-year exercise in taking ideas from philosophers and historians, mixing them with my own experience working in death, and attempting to make them, somehow, felt.

Many of the texts that had a huge influence are only cited briefly in the final book. Please visit the original texts, especially those of Ernest Becker, Philippe Ariès, Joseph Campbell, Caroline Walker Bynum, and Viktor Frankl. It will do wonders to advance your relationship with death and mortality.

While working at the crematorium I kept a secret blog called Salon of Souls, which caught me as I was in 2008, and didn't allow me to revise history.

I was fortunate in having the full support of my co-workers at the crematorium: Michael, Chris, and Bruce. Not only did they allow me to use their real names, they agreed to sit down for interviews and multiple follow-ups as the book was written. I hope my tremendous respect for these men and what they do comes across as you read.

Through the Order of the Good Death, I am lucky to know the best death academics and funeral professionals working today. Their access to resource libraries, real-world experience, and large pools of arcane and morbid knowledge has been invaluable.

AUTHOR'S NOTE

Becker, Ernest. *The Denial of Death*. New York: Simon & Schuster, 1973.
Wales, Henry G. 'Death Comes to Mata Hari.' International News Service, October 19, 1917.

SHAVING BYRON

Tennyson, Lord Alfred. *In Memoriam: An Authoritative Text*. New York: W. W. Norton & Company, 2004.

PUPPY SURPRISE

Ball, Katharine. 'Death Benefits.' *San Francisco Bay Guardian*, December 15, 1993.
Gorer, Geoffrey. 'The Pornography of Death.'

Encounter 5, no. 4 (1955): 49–52.

Iserson, Kenneth V. *Death to Dust? What Happens to Dead Bodies*. Galen Press, 1994.

Poe, Edgar Allan. 'Annabel Lee.' In *The Complete Stories and Poems of Edgar Allan Poe*. New York: Random House, 2012.

Solnit, Rebecca. *A Paradise Built in Hell: The Extraordinary Communities That Arise in Disaster*. New York: Penguin, 2010.

Suzuki, Hikaru. *The Price of Death: The Funeral Industry in Contemporary Japan*. Palo Alto, CA: Stanford University Press, 2000.

THE THUD

Campbell, Joseph. *The Hero with a Thousand Faces*. Princeton: Princeton University Press, 1973.

Doughty, Caitlin. 'Children & Death.' *Fortnight* (2011), fortnightjournal.com/caitlin-doughty/262-children-death.html.

Laderman, Gary. *The Sacred Remains: American Attitudes Toward Death, 1799–1883*. New Haven: Yale University Press, 1999.

May, Trevor. *The Victorian Undertaker*. Oxford, UK: Shire Publications Ltd, 1996.

Ariès, Philippe. *The Hour of Our Death*. Oxford: Oxford University Press, 1991.

Connolly, Ceci. 'A Grisly but Essential Issue.' *The Washington Post*, June 9, 2006.

Dante. *The Inferno*. Translated by Robert Hollander and Jean Hollander. New York: Anchor Books, 2002.

Orent, Wendy. *Plague: The Mysterious Past and Terrifying Future of the World's Most Dangerous Disease*. New York: Simon & Schuster, 2013.

Stackhouse, John. 'India's Turtles Clean Up the Ganges.' *Seattle Times*, October 1, 1992.

PUSH THE BUTTON

Bar-Yosef, Ofer. 'The Chronology of the Middle Paleolithic of the Levant.' In *Neandertals and Modern Humans in Western Asia*. New York: Plenum Press, 1998.

Chrisafis, Angelique. 'French Judge Closes Body Worlds-style Exhibition of Corpses.' *The Guardian*, April 21, 2009.

Cioran, Emil. *A Short History of Decay*. Arcade Publishing, 1975.

Grainger, Hilary J. *Death Redesigned: British Crematoria History, Architecture and*

Landscape. Spire Books, 2005.

Newberg, Andrew, and Eugene D'Aquili. *Why God Won't Go Away: Brain Science and the Biology of Belief.* New York: Random House, 2008.

Nietzsche, Friedrich Wilhelm. *Nietzsche: The Anti-Christ, Ecce Homo, Twilight of the Idols: And Other Writings.* Cambridge: Cambridge University Press, 2005.

Prothero, Stephen R. *Purified by Fire: A History of Cremation in America.* Berkeley: University of California Press, 2002.

Schwartz, Vanessa R. *Spectacular Realities: Early Mass Culture in Fin-de-siècle Paris.* Berkeley: University of California Press, 1999.

PINK COCKTAIL

Aoki, Shinmon. *Coffinman: The Journal of a Buddhist Mortician.* Buddhist Education Center, 2004.

Ash, Niema. *Flight of the Wind Horse: A Journal into Tibet.* London: Rider, 1992.

Beane Freeman, Laura, et al. 'Mortality from lymphohe-matopoietic malignancies among workers in formaldehyde industries: The National Cancer Institute Cohort.' *Journal of the National Cancer Institute* 101, no. 10 (2009): 751–61.

Conklin, Beth A. *Consuming Grief: Compassionate Cannibalism in an Amazonian Society.* University of Texas Press, 2001.

Geertz, Clifford. *The Interpretation of Cultures: Selected Essays.* New York: Basic Books, 1973.

Gilpin Faust, Drew. *The Republic of Suffering: Death and the American Civil War.* New York: Random House, 2009.

Habenstein, Robert W., and William M. Lamers. *The History of American Funeral Directing.* National Funeral Directors Association of the United States, 2007.

Laderman, Gary. *The Sacred Remains: American Attitudes Toward Death, 1799–1883.* New Haven: Yale University Press, 1996.

O'Neill, John. *Essaying Montaigne: A Study of the Renaissance Institution of Writing and Reading.* Liverpool: Liverpool University Press, 2001.

Taylor, John. *Death and the Afterlife in Ancient Egypt.* Chicago: University of Chicago Press, 2001.

DEMON BABIES

Baudelaire, Charles. *The Flowers of Evil* [Les fleurs du mal]. Translated by Christopher Thompson. iUniverse, 2000.

Cohan, Norman. *Europe's Inner Demons: The Demonization of Christians in Medieval Christendom*. New York: Penguin, 1977.

Kramer, Heinrich, and James Sprenger. *The Malleus Maleficarum*. Translated by Montague Summers. Courier Dover Publications, 2012.

Paré, Ambroise. *Des monstres et prodiges*. Librairie Droz, 2003.

Roper, Lyndal. *Witch Craze: Terror and Fantasy in Baroque Germany*. New Haven: Yale University Press, 2006.

Sanger, Carol. ''The Birth of Death': Stillborn Birth Certificates and the Problem for Law.' *California Law Review* 100, no. 269 (2012): 269–312.

DIRECT DISPOSAL

Gorer, Geoffrey. 'The Pornography of Death.' *Encounter* 5, no. 4 (1955): 49–52.

Mitford, Jessica. *The American Way of Death: Revisited*. New York: Random House, 2011.

———. Interview with Christopher Hitchens. The New York Public Library, 1988.

Prothero, Stephen R. *Purified by Fire: A History of Cremation in America*. Berkeley: University of California Press, 2002.

Time. 'The Necropolis: First Step Up to

Heaven.' *Time*, September 30, 1966.

Waugh, Evelyn. *The Loved One*. Boston: Back Bay Books, 2012.

UNNATURAL NATURAL

Snyder Sachs, Jessica. *Corpse: Nature, Forensics, and the Struggle to Pinpoint Time of Death*. Da Capo Press, 2002.

ALAS, POOR YORICK

Asma, Stephen T. *Stuffed Animals and Pickled Heads: The Culture and Evolution of Natural History Museums*. Oxford: Oxford University Press, 2003.

Friend, Tad. 'Jumpers: The Fatal Grandeur of the Golden Gate Bridge.' *The New Yorker*, October 13, 2003.

Harrison, Ann Tukey, editor. *The Danse Macabre of Women: Ms. Fr. 995 of the Bibliothèque Nationale*. Akron, OH: Kent State University Press, 1994.

Paglia, Camille. *Sexual Personae*. New Haven: Yale University Press, 1990.

Roach, Mary. *Stiff: The Curious Lives of Human Cadavers*. New York: W. W. Norton & Company, 2004.

Andersen, Hans Christian. *The Little Mermaid*. Translated by H. B. Paull. Planet, 2012.

Brothers Grimm. *The Grimm Reader: The Classic Tales of the Brothers Grimm*. Translated by Maria Tatar. New York: W. W. Norton & Company, 2010.

Bynum, Caroline Walker. *Jesus as Mother: Studies in the Spirituality of the High Middle Ages*. Berkeley: University of California Press, 1982.

Campbell, Joseph. *The Hero with a Thousand Faces*. Princeton: Princeton University Press, 1973.

Doughty, Caitlin. 'The Old & the Lonely.' *Fortnight* (2011), fortnightjournal.com/caitlin-doughty/276-the-old-the-lonely.html.

Lang, Andrew. *The Red True Story Book*. Longmans, Green, and Company, 1900.

Rank, Otto. *Beyond Psychology*. Courier Dover Publications, 2012.

Sachs, Adam. 'Stranger than Paradise.' *The New York Times Style Magazine*, May 10, 2013.

BUBBLATING

Ariès, Philippe. *The Hour of Our Death*. Oxford: Oxford University Press, 1991.

Campobasso, Carlo Pietro, Giancarlo Di Vella, and Francesco Introna. 'Factors affecting decomposition and Diptera colonization.' *Forensic Science International* 120 nos. 1–2 (2001): 18–27.

Dickey, Colin. *Afterlives of the Saints*. Unbridled Books, 2012.

Eberwine, Donna. 'Disaster Myths that Just Won't Die.' *Perspectives in Health — The Magazine of the Pan American Health Organization* 10, no. 1 (2005).

Geertz, Clifford. *The Religion of Java*. Chicago: University of Chicago Press, 1976.

Kanda, Fusae. 'Behind the Sensationalism: Images of a Decaying Corpse in Japanese Buddhist Art.' *Art Bulletin* 87, no. 1 (2005).

Lindsay, Suzanne G. *Funerary Arts and Tomb Cult: Living with the Dead in France, 1750–1870*. Ashgate Publishing, 2012.

Mirbeau, Octave. *Torture Garden*. Translated by Alvah Bessie. powerHouse Books, 2000.

Miller, William Ian. *The Anatomy of Disgust*. Cambridge, MA: Harvard University Press, 2009.

Mongillo, John F., and Bibi Booth. *Environmental Activists*. Greenwood Publishing Group, 2001.

Noble, Thomas F. X., and Thomas Head. *Soldiers of Christ: Saints and Saints' Lives from Late Antiquity and the Early Middle*

Ages. University Park, PA: Penn State Press, 2010.

Shelley, Mary. *Frankenstein*. London: Palgrave Macmillan, 2000.

GHUSL

Beckett, Samuel. *Waiting for Godot: A Tragicomedy in Two Acts*. London: Faber & Faber, 2012.

Bynum, Caroline Walker. *Fragmentation and Redemption: Essays on Gender and the Human Body in Medieval Religion*. Zone Books, 1991.

Metcalf, Peter, and Richard Huntington. *Celebrations of Death: The Anthropology of Mortuary Ritual*. Cambridge: Cambridge University Press, 1991.

Nelson, Walter. *Buddha: His Life and His Teachings*. New York: Penguin, 2008.

Quigley, Christine. *The Corpse: A History*. MacFarland, 2005.

THE REDWOODS

Frankl, Viktor Emil. *Man's Search for Meaning: An Introduction to Logotherapy*. Boston: Beacon Press, 1992.

Heinrich, Bernd. *Life Everlasting: The Animal Way of Death*. Boston: Houghton Mifflin Harcourt, 2012.

Walther, Ingo F. *Paul Gauguin, 1848–1903: The Primitive Sophisticate*. Taschen, 1999.

Wilson, Horace Hayman. *The Vishńu Puráńa: A System of Hindu Mythology and Tradition*. J. Murray, 1840.

DETH SKOOL

Collison, Tim. 'Cosmetic Considerations for the Infant Death.' *Dodge Magazine*, Winter 2009.

Lynch, Thomas. *The Undertaking: Life Studies from the Dismal Trade*. New York: W. W. Norton & Company, 2010.

THE ART OF DYING

Atkinson, David William. *The English Ars Moriendi*. Lang, 1992.

Campbell, Joseph. *The Hero with a Thousand Faces*. Princeton: Princeton University Press, 1973.

Colman, Penny. *Corpses, Coffins, and Crypts: A History of Burial*. Boston: Macmillan, 1997.

Gawande, Atul. 'The Way We Age Now.' *The New Yorker*, April 30, 2007.

Gollner, Adam Leith. 'The Immortality Financiers: The Billionaires Who Want to Live Forever.' *The Daily Beast*, August 20, 2013.

Hanson, Rick. *Buddha's Brain: The Practical Neuroscience of Happiness, Love, and Wisdom.* New Harbinger Publications, 2009.

Jacoby, Susan. *Never Say Die: The Myth and Marketing of the New Old Age.* New York: Random House, 2012.

Von Franz, Marie-Louise. 'Archetypal Experiences Surrounding Death.' Lecture, Panarion Conference, C. G. Jung Institute of Los Angeles, 1978.

PRODIGAL DAUGHTER:
AN EPILOGUE OF SORTS

Diggory, James C., and Doreen Z. Rothman. 'Values Destroyed by Death.' *The Journal of Abnormal and Social Psychology* 63, no. 1(1961): 205–10.

Louis C.K. *Chewed Up*. Filmed at the Berklee Performance Center, Boston, October 2008.

We do hope that you have enjoyed reading this large print book.

Did you know that all of our titles are available for purchase?

We publish a wide range of high quality large print books including:
Romances, Mysteries, Classics
General Fiction
Non Fiction and Westerns

Special interest titles available in large print are:
The Little Oxford Dictionary
Music Book
Song Book
Hymn Book
Service Book

Also available from us courtesy of Oxford University Press:
Young Readers' Dictionary
(large print edition)
Young Readers' Thesaurus
(large print edition)

For further information or a free brochure, please contact us at:
Ulverscroft Large Print Books Ltd.,
The Green, Bradgate Road, Anstey,
Leicester, LE7 7FU, England.
Tel: (00 44) 0116 236 4325
Fax: (00 44) 0116 234 0205

Other titles published by Ulverscroft:

SHOP GIRL

Mary Portas

Young Mary Newton, born into a large Irish family in a small Watford semi, is always getting into trouble. When she isn't choking back fits of giggles at Holy Communion or eating Chappie dog food for a bet, she's accidentally setting fire to the local school. Whilst money is scarce, these are good times, and everything revolves around the force of nature that is Theresa, Mary's mum. But when tragedy unexpectedly blows this world apart, a new chapter in Mary's life opens up. She takes to the camp and glamour of Harrods window dressing like a duck to water — and Mary, Queen of Shops is born . . .

TSUNAMI KIDS

Paul Forkan and Rob Forkan

Siblings Rob, Paul, Mattie and Rosie were orphaned in the 2004 Boxing Day tsunami. They subsequently made a harrowing 200km trek across the devastated country of Sri Lanka, trying to discover the fate of their parents. The bravery and ingenuity they displayed was a direct result of their unique upbringing. Taken out of school at a young age, they had received an unconventional global education, learning independence and emotional resilience . . . Almost a decade after the disaster, the eldest brothers, Rob and Paul, created the multinational brand Gandys, and established the charitable foundation Orphans for Orphans. This is the story of their journey from survival to success.

STALIN'S HAD IT NOW!

James Stevenson

'So you lot want to be pilots? Bloody hell, Stalin's had it now!' Such were the withering words of the corporal as he eyed his raw National Service recruits. When young James Stevenson was called up in 1952, he knew exactly how he wished to serve his country — flying in the RAF. From his very first flight in a Tiger Moth ('Excuse me, sir, where are the brakes?') to mock dogfights with his fellow trainees (strictly forbidden), square-bashing and Brasso-ing in England to spinning aerobatics over the snowy prairies of Canada, this is the story of James's quest for his coveted wings.

FREDERICK DOUGLASS IN IRELAND

Laurence Fenton

In the summer of 1845, a man named Frederick Douglass disembarked ship in Dublin. It marked the start of a two-year lecture tour of Britain and Ireland by the celebrated author, orator — and escaped slave. Advised to leave America for his own safety after the publication of his eloquent and incendiary abolitionist memoir, Douglass proceeded to spend four months in Ireland describing and denouncing the horrors of slavery: packing full halls with his oratorical skill; sharing a stage with 'The Liberator' Daniel O'Connell; and taking the pledge from 'The Apostle of Temperance' Fr. Theobald Mathew.